5th Workshop on Structured Prediction for NLP (SPNLP 2021)

Held online due to COVID-19

Bangkok, Thailand
6 August 2021

ISBN: 978-1-7138-3387-1

SPNLP 2021

The 5th Workshop on Structured Prediction for NLP

Proceedings of the Workshop

August 6th, 2021
Bangkok, Thailand (online)

Introduction

Welcome to the Fifth Workshop on Structured Prediction for NLP!

Structured prediction has a strong tradition within the natural language processing (NLP) community, owing to the discrete, compositional nature of words and sentences, which leads to natural combinatorial representations such as trees, sequences, segments, or alignments, among others. It is no surprise that structured output models have been successful and popular in NLP applications since their inception. Many other NLP tasks, including, but not limited to: semantic parsing, slot filling, machine translation, or information extraction, are commonly modeled as structured problems, and accounting for said structure has often lead to performance gain.

This workshop follows the four previous successful editions in 2020, 2019, 2017 and 2016 on Structured Prediction for NLP, as well as the closely related ICML 17 Workshop on Deep Structured Prediction. This year we received 18 submissions and, after double-blind peer review, 10 were accepted (2 of which are non-archival papers) for presentation in this edition of the workshop, all exploring this interplay between structure and neural data representations, from different, important points of view. The program includes work on structure-informed representation learning, leveraging structure in problems like parsing, hierarchical classification, etc. and structured feedback for sequence-to-sequence models. Our program also includes six invited presentations from influential researchers.

Our warmest thanks go to the program committee – for their time and effort providing valuable feedback, to all submitting authors – for their thought-provoking work, and to the invited speakers – for doing us the honor of joining our program.

We are profoundly saddened by the loss of Arzoo Katiyar, who was our beloved program committee member since many previous editions. Our deepest condolences to her family and friends.

Zornitsa Kozareva
Sujith Ravi
Priyanka Agrawal
André Martins
Andreas Vlachos

Organizing Committee

Zornitsa Kozareva, Facebook AI, USA
Sujith Ravi, SliceX AI, USA
Priyanka Agrawal, Booking.com, Netherlands
André F. T. Martins, Instituto Superior Técnico, Instituto de Telecomunicações, and Unbabel, Portugal
Andreas Vlachos, University of Cambridge, UK

Program Committee

Heng Ji, University of Illinois Urbana-Champaign, USA
Vivek Srikumar, University of Utah, USA
Roi Reichart, Technion - Israel Institute of Technology, Israel
Kevin Gimpel, TTI Chicago, USA
Ivan Titov, University of Edinburgh, Scotland
Wilker Aziz, University of Amsterdam, Netherlands
Hiko Schamoni, Heidelberg University, Germany
Arzoo Katiyar, Cornell University, USA
Tianze Shi, Cornell University, USA
Sabrina Mielke, Johns Hopkins University, USA
Pranava Madhyastha, Imperial College London, UK
Amr Sharaf, University of Maryland, USA
Tim Vieira, Johns Hopkins University, USA
Parag Jain, University of Edinburgh, UK
Sean Welleck, New York University, USA
Michail Korakakis, University of Cambridge, UK
Ran Zmigrod, University of Cambridge, UK
Chunchuan Lyu, University of Edinburgh, UK
Parisa Kordjamshidi,Michigan State University, USA
Julius Cheng, University of Cambridge, UK
Patrick Fernandes, Instituto Superior Técnico, Portugal, and Carnegie Mellon University, USA

Invited Speakers

Heng Ji, University of Illinois Urbana-Champaign
Rada Mihalcea, University of Michigan
Scott Wen-tau Yih, Facebook AI Research
Carolin Lawrence, NEC Labs Europe
Iryna Gurevych, Technical University of Darmstadt

Table of Contents

Conference Program

6th August 2021

0900–0910   *Opening Remarks*

09:10–09:50   *Invited Talk 1*
Iryna Gurevych (Technical University Darmstadt, Germany)

09:50–10:30   *Invited Talk 2*
Carolin Lawrence (NEC Labs Europe, Germany)

10:30–10:40   *Break*

10:40–11:40   *Poster Session I*

RewardsOfSum: Exploring Reinforcement Learning Rewards for Summarisation
Jacob Parnell, Inigo Jauregi Unanue and Massimo Piccardi

SmBoP: Semi-autoregressive Bottom-up Semantic Parsing
Ohad Rubin and Jonathan Berant

11:40–12:20   *Invited Talk 3*
Rada Mihalcea (University of Michigan, USA)

12:20–12:35   *Learning compositional structures for semantic graph parsing*
Jonas Groschwitz, Meaghan Fowlie and Alexander Koller

12:35–12:50   *Offline Reinforcement Learning from Human Feedback in Real-World Sequence-to-Sequence Tasks*
Julia Kreutzer, Stefan Riezler and Carolin Lawrence

12:50–13:50   *Break*

13:50–14:30   *Invited Talk 4*
Heng Ji (University of Illinois Urbana-Champaign, USA)

6th August 2021 (continued)

14:30–14:45   *Mode recovery in neural autoregressive sequence modeling*
Ilia Kulikov, Sean Welleck and Kyunghyun Cho

14:45–15:45   **Poster Session II**

Using Hierarchical Class Structure to Improve Fine-Grained Claim Classification
Erenay Dayanik, Andre Blessing, Nico Blokker, Sebastian Haunss, Jonas Kuhn,
Gabriella Lapesa and Sebastian Padó

A Globally Normalized Neural Model for Semantic Parsing
Chenyang Huang, Wei Yang, Yanshuai Cao, Osmar Zaïane and Lili Mou

15:45–16:15   **Break**

16:15–16:30   *Comparing Span Extraction Methods for Semantic Role Labeling*
Zhisong Zhang, Emma Strubell and Eduard Hovy

16:30–17:10   *Invited Talk 5*
Scott Wen-tau Yih (Facebook AI Research, USA)

17:10–17:20   ***Closing Remarks***

RewardsOfSum: Exploring Reinforcement Learning Rewards for Summarisation

Jacob Parnell[1,2], Inigo Jauregi Unanue[1,2], Massimo Piccardi[1]
[1]University of Technology Sydney, NSW, Australia
[2]RoZetta Technology, NSW, Australia
{jacob.parnell,inigo.jauregi}@rozettatechnology.com
massimo.piccardi@uts.edu.au

Abstract

To date, most abstractive summarisation models have relied on variants of the negative log-likelihood (NLL) as their training objective. In some cases, reinforcement learning has been added to train the models with an objective that is closer to their evaluation measures (e.g. ROUGE). However, the reward function to be used within the reinforcement learning approach can play a key role for performance and is still partially unexplored. For this reason, in this paper, we propose two reward functions for the task of abstractive summarisation: the first function, referred to as *RwB-Hinge*, dynamically selects the samples for the gradient update. The second function, nicknamed *RISK*, leverages a small pool of strong candidates to inform the reward. In the experiments, we probe the proposed approach by fine-tuning an NLL pre-trained model over nine summarisation datasets of diverse size and nature. The experimental results show a consistent improvement over the negative log-likelihood baselines.

1 Introduction

The current state-of-the-art neural text summarisation models have been refined to excel at either the extractive or abstractive styles, or even both (Zhang et al., 2020a; Lewis et al., 2020; Raffel et al., 2020). Along with contemporary summarisation datasets (Narayan et al., 2018a; Grusky et al., 2018; Fabbri et al., 2019), the advent of large pre-trained language models, and their subsequent derivations (Liu and Lapata, 2019; Park, 2020), has allowed summarisation to become a more practical and reasonable task to implement, without compromising, and often improving, the accuracy. However, these models usually employ the standard negative log-likelihood (NLL) as their training objective, which aims to maximise the likelihood of each token in a given ground-truth reference. Despite its efficacy, the NLL fails to account for synonymous tokens and other potentially valid variations, and strongly biases the model towards the ground-truth reference (Ranzato et al., 2016). Furthermore, the NLL operates as a token-level objective during training, which promotes an inconsistent comparison with sequence-level evaluation metrics, such as ROUGE (Lin, 2004).

In order to address the inconsistency between token-level training and sequence-level evaluation, reinforcement learning (RL) has been adopted in summarisation and other language generation tasks to afford the optimization of sequence-level metrics during training (Paulus et al., 2018; Pasunuru and Bansal, 2018). Reinforcement learning has proved successful at improving the accuracy of language generation tasks, such as summarisation (Paulus et al., 2018; Arumae and Liu, 2018; Pasunuru and Bansal, 2018) and machine translation (Ranzato et al., 2016; Edunov et al., 2018). However, balancing exploration and exploitation remains imperative to the successful choice of an effective reward. When standard RL techniques, such as REINFORCE (Williams, 1992), are implemented in natural language generation tasks, the required expectation becomes intractable due to large vocabulary sizes. Therefore, the application of REINFORCE is typically reduced to calculating the approximate expectation with respect to only a single predicted sequence. To teach the model to understand the importance of sample variation among synonymous tokens, we instead choose to implement an objective function which includes multiple predicted sequences, allowing for a scenario in which several valid candidate summaries can be considered. Another consideration is that the success of techniques such as REINFORCE strongly depends on the use of an effective and appropriate reward. Designing such a reward, one which enables the model to manipulate multiple

1

Proceedings of the 5th Workshop on Structured Prediction for NLP, pages 1–11
August 1–6, 2021. ©2021 Association for Computational Linguistics

sequences and yet provides a positive and informative outcome in the process, is therefore necessary for producing better results. This allows us to modify the reinforcement learning framework in such a way that enforces only a higher weighting to those predicted sequences which obtain a higher reward. As such, we apply two techniques to summarisation; *RwB-Hinge*, which applies a hinge-loss modification to the classical REINFORCE with baseline (Rennie et al., 2017) to selectively apply the model gradients, and *Expected Risk Minimization (RISK)* (Edunov et al., 2018), which leverages a small pool of strong sampled candidates to smartly inform the reward function. We aptly refer to our framework as *RewardsOfSum*, to hint at the exploration of suitable reward functions for summarisation. Empirically, we show that the two proposed variants perform better than standard negative log-likelihood baselines over a range of datasets of diverse size and nature.

2 Related Work

In recent years, there has been some work in summarisation to separate from the traditional negative log-likelihood (NLL) objective function, and mollify its dependency on ground-truth references. Several implementations of reinforcement learning in summarisation involved optimizing discrete metrics, such as the standard ROUGE (Paulus et al., 2018; Narayan et al., 2018b). Others have introduced novel rewards into the reinforcement learning framework, such as question-focused rewards (Arumae and Liu, 2018), saliency and entailment rewards (Pasunuru and Bansal, 2018), and even distributional semantic rewards (Li et al., 2019). Gao et al. (2020) also present a novel unsupervised metric for summarisation which correlates highly with discrete evaluation metrics if adopted in a reinforcement learning approach.

On the other hand, there has been much work in leveraging large, pre-trained language models (LM) (Devlin et al., 2019; Lewis et al., 2020; Raffel et al., 2020) to improve the quality and performance of summarisation models. Utilizing pre-trained language models requires significantly less engineering effort to continually improve over state-of-the-art baselines. Typically, these approaches include using novel pre-training objectives (Zhang et al., 2020a; Raffel et al., 2020; Zhu et al., 2020) or implementing successful reinforcement learning techniques (Bae et al., 2019). Li et al. (2019) found

that optimizing semantic rewards in reinforcement learning, using BERTScore (Zhang et al., 2020b), does not necessarily correlate with the ROUGE score at test time. As such, the choice of reward in a reinforcement learning approach should attempt to carefully align with the evaluation metric.

How best to inform the reward via the reward function, is critical to the performance of models in an RL framework. In our work, we aim to stray from the typical sole NLL objective, and by leveraging a pre-trained language model in a reinforcement learning framework, explore different RL-based reward functions for summarisation.

3 Proposed Reinforcement Learning Training

In order to improve over the negative log-likelihood baseline models, we aim to implement a reinforcement learning framework that adopts the standard evaluation metric, ROUGE, as a reward during training. We aim to keep consistent with previous implementations of reinforcement learning in summarisation, and assume ROUGE-L F1 to be the reward metric in the following work.

In Sections 3.1 and 3.2, we consider the following standard notations: x is defined as an input source document, y^*, $\hat{y}$, and y^s are referred to as the ground-truth reference, argmax prediction, and sampled sequence, respectively, and $r(y)$ refers to the reward of sequence y, computed with respect to the ground-truth reference, y^*. By exploiting a combination of sampling and predictions, we aim to enhance training diversity in the vein of the work of Li and Jurafsky (2016); Li et al. (2016); Holtzman et al. (2020).

3.1 RwB-Hinge

We adopt the standard self-critical policy gradient objective (Rennie et al., 2017), notably applied to summarisation by Paulus et al. (2018):

$$\alpha = -[r(y^s) - r(\hat{y})] \qquad (1)$$

$$L_{RwB} = \alpha \sum_{t=1}^{n'} \log p(y_t^s | y_1, \ldots, y_{t-1}, x) \qquad (2)$$

In (1), y^s and $\hat{y}$ denote a sampled sequence and the argmax prediction of the current model, respectively. The reward of the argmax, $r(\hat{y})$, is used as a "baseline" for the reward of the sample, $r(y^s)$. It is easy to see that if $r(y^s) - r(\hat{y}) > 0$, the sign of this loss is negative, treating y^s as a "good" prediction and leading to an increase of its probability. Conversely, if the sign is positive, y^s is deemed as a "bad" prediction and its probability is decreased.

However, in abstractive summarisation it is not trivial to discriminate between a good and a bad summary when the reward score is in an intermediate range. To avoid inappropriately penalising acceptable predictions, we propose incorporating a hinge loss in (1):

$$\alpha = -\max\left[0, (r(y^s) - r(\hat{y}))\right] \qquad (3)$$

The hinge loss allows the model to limit the gradient updates to only the predictions that are considered as good. In this way, we avoid the risk of unstable training updates and hope to afford a clearer trajectory towards a well-trained model.

3.2 Expected RISK Minimization

We also utilise a classical structured loss function that has been shown to perform well in sequence-to-sequence learning tasks (Edunov et al., 2018):

$$L_{RISK} = \sum_{y \in U(x)} -r(y) \cdot p(y|x, \theta) \qquad (4)$$

In (4), y represents one of multiple candidate summaries, sampled or predicted with the methods defined in Section 4.2 (e.g. argmax, Gumbel-Softmax (Jang et al., 2017)), that form the total candidate summary set $U(x)$. The conditional probability of the predicted summary is noted as $p(y|x, \theta)$.

This conditional probability is defined in (5), where m is the number of tokens in the summary. The sum of logarithms in (6) is divided by the total number of tokens in the sequence, and is scaled back using an exponential function, allowing each candidate summary to be compared fairly in the objective function and avoiding underflow.

$$p(y|x, \theta) = \frac{f(y, x, \theta)}{\sum\limits_{y' \in U(x)} f(y', x, \theta)} \qquad (5)$$

$$\eta = \sum_{j=1}^{m} \log p(u^j | u^1, \ldots, u^{j-1}, x, \theta) \qquad (6)$$

$$f(y, x, \theta) = \exp\left[\frac{\eta}{m}\right] \qquad (7)$$

By using this objective function, the model is taught to assign higher probability to the candidate summaries that obtain higher rewards. This objective does not require a baseline or hinge loss to select the predictions, since using multiple candidates already exposes the model to different, potentially valid predictions. Edunov et al. (2018) demonstrates the effectiveness of this approach at sentence level for both neural machine translation and summarisation. For the summarisation task, Edunov et al. (2018) compute the reward at sentence-level since their dataset has single-sentence references. However, as the reward function is agnostic to single or multi-sentence predictions, we can easily translate the *RISK* objective function to be used at summary level.

3.3 Overall Training Objective

Similar to previous reinforcement learning implementations (Paulus et al., 2018; Li et al., 2019), we, too, utilise a mixed learning objective function, as shown in (8). This mixed approach helps the model to not deviate too much from the reference summaries, given a γ balancing coefficient chosen with a strict validation criterion (Appendix A). The L_{RL} term refers to either the RwB-Hinge or RISK training objective function.

$$L_{mixed} = \gamma L_{XENT} + (1 - \gamma) L_{RL} \qquad (8)$$

4 Experimental Setup

4.1 Datasets

Inspired by the recent work from Zhang et al. (2020a), we utilise nine of the summarisation datasets reported in their paper. The nine datasets have been chosen based on the different lengths of their reference summaries, to provide enough of a variation to demonstrate the applicability of the presented methods. We split the datasets into three classes: "short", "medium", and "long". Short datasets have reference summaries ≤ 64 tokens, medium datasets > 64 and ≤ 128 tokens, and long datasets > 128 tokens.

4.2 Sampling Methods

In order to promote exploration across the vocabulary distribution, we employ three simple methodologies to provide candidate sequences for our training objectives.

Argmax: As is the standard with the majority of sequence generation tasks, a predicted sentence

Dataset	Train	Test	Dev
AESLC	14.4K	1.9K	1.9K
Gigaword	3.8M	1.9K	189K
XSum	203K	11.3K	11.3K
CNN/DM	287K	11.4K	13.3K
Reddit-TIFU	33.7K	4.2K	4.2K
Newsroom	995K	108K	108K
Pubmed	119K	6.6K	6.6K
ArXiv	203K	6.4K	6.4K
Billsum	18.9K	3.2K	1.2K

Table 1: Statistics on the datasets used in the experiments. Figures are rounded. The top third are short datasets (≤ 64 tokens references summaries), the middle third are medium datasets (> 64 and ≤ 128 tokens), and the bottom third are long datasets (> 128 tokens).

can be easily provided by allowing the model to make hard decisions (e.g. argmax) over the probability distribution generated by the decoder. This allows us to use it as a baseline for the following experiments. In its simplest form the argmax is defined as:

$$\hat{y}_j = \operatorname*{argmax}_{y} p(y|x, y_{j-1}^*, \theta) \quad j = 1, \ldots, n \quad (9)$$

where we use "teacher forcing" for the predictions.

2nd-Best: Similar to the argmax, we employ a k-best approach to sample the second best-argmax from the same probability distribution generated by the decoder. This allows us to choose different, yet similarly weighted words from the decoder to introduce variability between produced summaries:

$$y_j^s = \operatorname*{argmax}_{k=2} p(y|x, y_{j-1}^*, \theta) \quad j = 1, \ldots, n$$
$$(10)$$

Gumbel-Softmax: We also utilise a recent reparameterization technique known as the Gumbel-Softmax (Jang et al., 2017) that allows sampling soft latent categorical variables by transforming samples from a Gumbel distribution. Compared to the standard "hard" predictions, this approach is differentiable and allows controlling the sparsity of the samples by a temperature parameter, τ:

$$\tilde{p}_j^i = \frac{\exp((\log(p_j^i) + g^i)/\tau}{\sum_{v=1}^{V} \exp((\log(p_j^v) + g^v)/\tau} \quad (11)$$

In (11), g^i is a sample from the zero-mean, unit-scale Gumbel distribution, p_j^i is the probability dis-

tribution for a given token i at slot j, and the temperature parameter, τ, controls the sparsity of the output soft variable, $\tilde{p}_j^i$. In our experiments, we have set τ to 0.1 to enforce sparsity.

4.3 Baseline Model and Training Runs

The abstractive text summarisation model we use for our experiments is PEGASUS, a large pretrained Transformer encoder-decoder architecture that has recently reported state-of-the-art results over a number of datasets. Please refer to Zhang et al. (2020a) for details. All hyperparameters used in our experiments can be found in Appendix B.

We employ two training approaches to test the solidity of the proposed methods. The first is a few-shot learning approach that adopts limited, fixed numbers of training samples (1000) and training iterations (2000) for fine-tuning the model. The second is a full-data learning approach, that utilises all available training data, and exhausts the objective function until convergence over the validation set. In all experiments, we first fine-tune a pretrained PEGASUS model with the NLL, and then we further fine-tune the NLL model with one of the proposed approaches. We train the model in this way to avoid the slow and inefficient training often associated with policy gradient objectives, and as a result, adhere to the standard warm-start NLL training adopted in previous reinforcement learning-based approaches (Paulus et al., 2018; Li et al., 2019).

In the following experiments, we refer to PEGASUS as PEG, and its NLL-tuned models with the suffixes -few_shot and -full_data. The proposed approaches are in turn noted as *RwB-Hinge* and *RISK*.

Experiment	Arg-max	2nd-Best	G-S
RwB-Hinge	✓		✓
RISK-2	✓		✓
RISK-3	✓	✓	✓

Table 2: Different experiments and the different sampling methods used in each. Here, *RISK-2* and *RISK-3* denote the number of samples we utilise in the RISK objective function; two and three, respectively.

5 Results

Tables 3, 4, and 5 show the results of each method in comparison to the NLL-tuned baseline for the nine reported datasets. Each table reports the

Model	AESLC			Gigaword			XSum		
	R-1	**R-2**	**R-L**	**R-1**	**R-2**	**R-L**	**R-1**	**R-2**	**R-L**
PEG$_{\text{few_shot}}$	**29.96**	**14.54**	**29.17**	31.81	13.19	29.12	41.81	18.32	33.50
+ *RwB-Hinge*	28.69	13.83	27.82	31.83	13.15	29.08	42.47†	18.82†	33.94†
+ *RISK-2*	29.35	14.14	28.39	31.96	13.22	29.27	42.57†	18.71†	33.96†
+ *RISK-3*	29.28	14.05	28.31	**32.10†**	**13.35†**	**29.43†**	**42.66†**	**19.01†**	**34.15†**
PEG$_{\text{full_data}}$	32.63	15.84	32.19	33.81	14.26	30.89	41.52	18.21	33.31
+ *RwB-Hinge*	**34.39†**	**17.58†**	**33.71†**	**34.10†**	**14.52**	**31.31†**	42.87†	**19.36**	34.56†
+ *RISK-2*	33.55†	17.01†	32.91†	33.97	14.45	31.18†	**42.93†**	19.25†	**34.67†**
+ *RISK-3*	33.75†	17.03†	33.04†	33.97	**14.52**	31.14†	42.74†	19.23†	34.60†

Table 3: Results on short datasets: AESLC, Gigaword, and XSum. Here we compare the limited resource (PEG$_{\text{few_shot}}$) and full-data (PEG$_{\text{full_data}}$) approaches with our different implementations. (†) means that the differences are statistically significant with respect to the baseline with a p-value < 0.05 over a bootstrap hypothesis test. Best ROUGE-1/2/L scores are bolded.

Model	CNN/DM			Reddit-TIFU			Newsroom		
	R-1	**R-2**	**R-L**	**R-1**	**R-2**	**R-L**	**R-1**	**R-2**	**R-L**
PEG$_{\text{few_shot}}$	40.65	17.60	37.81	24.84	7.21	20.12	33.33	20.01	29.17
+ *RwB-Hinge*	40.44	17.44	37.54	25.55†	7.23	20.09	34.03†	20.74†	29.86†
+ *RISK-2*	40.52	17.48	37.62	25.69†	7.25	20.26	34.26†	21.10†	30.14†
+ *RISK-3*	**40.76**	**17.63**	**37.87**	**25.73†**	**7.30**	**20.35**	**34.40†**	**21.27†**	**30.21†**
PEG$_{\text{full_data}}$	40.58	**18.15**	37.94	23.66	6.72	19.24	36.39	23.90	32.50
+ *RwB-Hinge*	40.84†	17.74	38.19†	23.95†	6.93	19.69†	**36.85†**	**24.01**	**33.00†**
+ *RISK-2*	**40.88†**	17.91	38.19†	24.25†	7.19†	20.00†	36.74	**24.01**	32.73
+ *RISK-3*	**40.88†**	17.91	**38.28†**	**24.70†**	**7.46†**	**20.25†**	36.04	23.22	32.18

Table 4: Results on medium datasets: CNN/DM, Reddit-TIFU, and Newsroom. Here we compare the limited resource (PEG$_{\text{few_shot}}$) and full-data (PEG$_{\text{full_data}}$) approaches with our different implementations. (†) means that the differences are statistically significant with respect to the baseline with a p-value < 0.05 over a bootstrap hypothesis test. Best ROUGE-1/2/L scores are bolded.

Model	Pubmed			ArXiv			Billsum		
	R-1	**R-2**	**R-L**	**R-1**	**R-2**	**R-L**	**R-1**	**R-2**	**R-L**
PEG$_{\text{few_shot}}$	38.28	13.70	23.32	38.08	11.61	22.87	48.27	27.79	35.70
+ *RwB-Hinge*	40.11†	14.45†	23.88†	38.85†	11.90†	22.88	48.61†	**29.35†**	**36.91†**
+ *RISK-2*	**40.19†**	**14.61†**	**23.98†**	**38.98†**	**12.02†**	**22.90**	48.21	28.34†	35.97
+ *RISK-3*	**40.19†**	14.55†	23.95†	38.68†	11.88†	22.81	**48.65**	28.71†	36.37†
PEG$_{\text{full_data}}$	40.57	16.05	**25.46**	38.48	13.33	24.12	52.98	34.44	41.36
+ *RwB-Hinge*	**40.80**	**16.27**	25.41	**38.95†**	**13.69†**	**24.19**	**54.30†**	**36.01†**	**42.76†**
+ *RISK-2*	40.32	15.85	25.31	38.76	13.55	24.11	53.76†	35.54†	42.37†
+ *RISK-3*	40.36	15.89	25.26	38.42	13.37	24.12	54.27†	35.80†	42.51†

Table 5: Results on long datasets: Pubmed, ArXiv, and Billsum. Here we compare the limited resource (PEG$_{\text{few_shot}}$) and full-data (PEG$_{\text{full_data}}$) approaches with our different implementations. (†) means that the differences are statistically significant with respect to the baseline with a p-value < 0.05 over a bootstrap hypothesis test. Best ROUGE-1/2/L scores are bolded.

few-shot (top halves) and full-data results (bottom halves), where the scores have been averaged over three independently-initialised training runs. Each fine-tuning method is employed in a mixed loss framework, as mentioned in (8) in Section 3.3; the value for the γ hyperparameter has been de-termined over the validation set as described in Appendix A. The results show that all the fine-tuning methods have surpassed the NLL baselines for almost all datasets. Several of these improvements have also passed a bootstrap test for statistical significance, which is regarded as a more appropriate

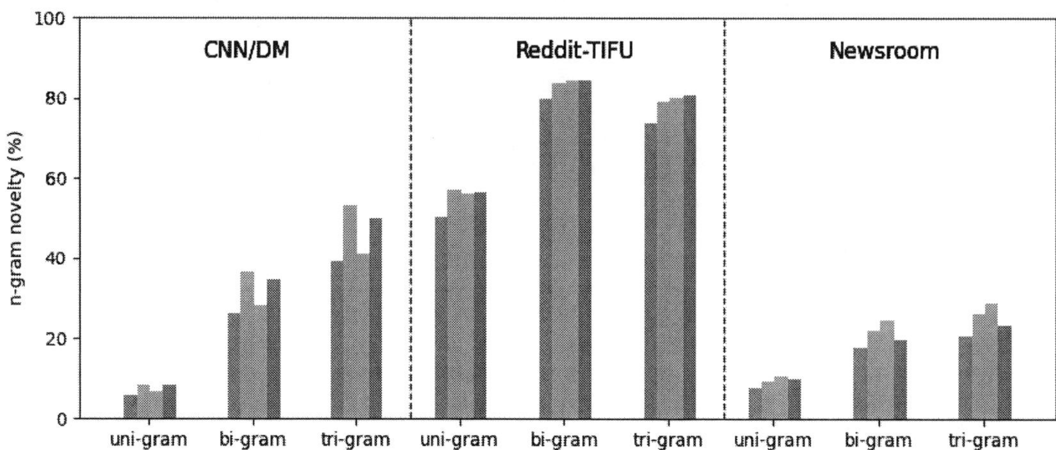

Figure 1: Comparing the uni-, bi-, and tri-gram novelty for the medium sized datasets. These datasets contain generated sequences up to 128 tokens in length. The methods are as follows: **NLL (baseline)**, *RwB-Hinge*, *RISK-2*, and *RISK-3*. The unique average n-gram novelty (n-grams that do not appear in the source text) is shown to increase across the board compared to the standard NLL baseline.

statistical test for summarisation compared to a t-test (Dror et al., 2018).

Figure 1 compares the effect that each fine-tuning method has had over the production of novel n-grams during test time (a property nicknamed as *n-gram novelty*). For medium sized datasets in particular, the reinforcement learning approaches appear to, on average, facilitate the production of more distinct uni-, bi-, and tri-grams at test time, compared to the NLL baseline. Whilst n-gram novelty is typically used in summarisation to showcase test-time summary abstractiveness, the results in Figure 1 highlight that training with objectives that promote sample variation leads to models capable of producing more novel n-grams (up to 13.8 pp in tri-gram novelty over CNN/DM). This is supported by the qualitative example in Table 6 which shows that the proposed fine-tuning methods can achieve greater diversity of summary predictions, whilst still improving over the baseline NLL ROUGE scores. It seems that the proposed fine-tuning methods have allowed the model to effectively weigh the predicted summaries during training, and when combined with the "stable" NLL in a mixed-loss approach, this has been able to produce well-rounded predictions, diverse enough to stray from the original baseline and the reference summaries.

In addition, Figure 2 shows a performance comparison with respect to the length of the reference summaries for the full-data approach over a medium size dataset (CNN/DM). We see that our fine-tuning methods have led, on average, to higher

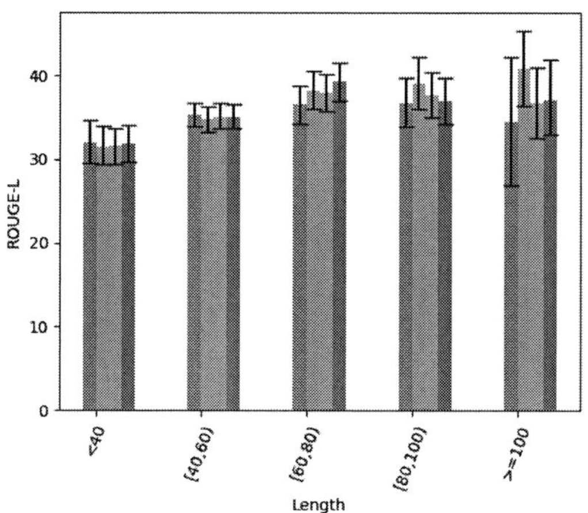

Figure 2: Comparison of each method for the full-data approach over a medium size dataset (CNN/DM). The methods are as follows: **NLL (baseline)**, *RwB-Hinge*, *RISK-2*, and *RISK-3*. We see that the reinforcement learning approaches have led, on average, to higher ROUGE-L scores for the longer summaries compared to the NLL baseline.

ROUGE-L scores for the longer summaries (up to 2.3 ROUGE-L points for summaries between 80-100 tokens, and up to 6.2 points for summaries over 100 tokens). Likely, the proposed methods have been able to amend the reported tendency of the NLL models to curtail the prediction of long summaries.

Comparing multiple fine-tuning methods is useful for showcasing the improvements that reinforcement learning can play on a generation task

Source Document
Dougie Freedman is on the verge of agreeing a new two-year deal to remain at Nottingham Forest. Freedman has stabilised Forest since he replaced cult hero Stuart Pearce and the club's owners are pleased with the job he has done at the City Ground. Dougie Freedman is set to sign a new deal at Nottingham Forest. Freedman has impressed at the City Ground since replacing Stuart Pearce in February. They made an audacious attempt on the play-off places when Freedman replaced Pearce but have tailed off in recent weeks. That has not prevented Forest's ownership making moves to secure Freedman on a contract for the next two seasons.

Reference
Nottingham Forest are close to extending Dougie Freedman's contract. The Forest boss took over from former manager Stuart Pearce in February. Freedman has since lead the club to ninth in the Championship.

NLL (40.00/30.43/32.85)
Dougie Freedman set to sign new deal at Nottingham Forest. Freedman has stabilised Forest since he replaced Stuart Pearce. Forest's owners are pleased with Freedman's job.

RwB-Hinge (49.00/36.24/34.43)
Dougie Freedman **is** set to sign **a** new **two-year** deal at Nottingham Forest. **The City Ground boss** has stabilised **the club** since he replaced Stuart Pearce. Forest's owners are pleased with Freedman's job at **the club**.

RISK-2 (50.66/44.59/44.00)
Dougie Freedman set to sign **a** new **two-year** deal at Nottingham Forest. Freedman has stabilised Forest since he replaced Stuart Pearce **in February**. Forest **made an audacious attempt at the play-off places when** Freedman replaced Pearce.

RISK-3 (49.33/40.54/40.00)
Dougie Freedman set to sign new deal at Nottingham Forest. Freedman has stabilised **the club** since he replaced Stuart Pearce **in February**. **The club's** owners are pleased with **the** job Freedman has **done at the City Ground**.

Table 6: Example of the performance of each method from the CNN/DailyMail dataset for the full-data approach, compared to the reference summary and NLL baseline. Words highlighted in blue indicate that they are not present in the baseline NLL summary. Here we choose a typical method that aligns the best with the average NLL baseline score, and compare how the methods pit against it. We see that there is a relative increase in ROUGE scores, whilst diversifying the output.

Dataset	Approach	RwB-Hinge	RISK-2	RISK-3
XSum (short)	Few-Shot	43.90/20.18/35.59	**44.03**/20.28/35.75	43.80/**20.30/35.76**
	Full-Data	42.97/19.45/34.73	42.92/**19.53**/34.73	**43.23**/19.25/**35.06**
Newsroom (medium)	Few-Shot	35.47/22.31/31.11	**36.20/23.11/31.81**	35.96/22.87/31.62
	Full-Data	**38.17/25.37/34.12**	37.02/24.36/33.21	37.08/25.11/33.22
Billsum (long)	Few-Shot	49.08/**29.96/37.63**	48.19/28.84/36.68	**49.23**/29.62/37.06
	Full-Data	**54.48/36.49/43.43**	53.51/35.24/42.49	54.10/35.39/42.50

Table 7: Scores on the validation set for short, medium, and long datasets to determine the best method for each size class. *RISK*, on average, appears to work best for short/medium sized datasets (up to 128 tokens), and *RwB-Hinge* works better for longer datasets (over 128 tokens).

Dataset	RwB: No Hinge-Loss	RwB: with Hinge-Loss
XSum (short)	42.82/19.32/34.43	**42.97/19.45/34.73**
Newsroom (medium)	**38.97/26.38/35.00**	38.17/25.37/34.12
Billsum (long)	53.04/34.87/42.14	**54.48/36.49/43.43**

Table 8: Comparisons between REINFORCE with baseline with and without the hinge-loss modification on the validation set for short, medium, and long datasets, to validate the use of the hinge-loss modification in our method. This is run over the full-data baselines, and shows that for the majority of dataset classes, the adopted hinge-loss modification leads to improvements in performance.

like summarisation. However, no single method has outperformed all others over all the datasets and in both the few-shot and full-data approaches. Whilst all methods have achieved interesting improvements over the baseline figures, we have run a comparison over the validation set to see if their relative rankings could be a reliable indicator of the relative rankings of the test set scores reported in

Tables 3, 4, and 5. Table 7 shows the results for one dataset per class size, showing that for the short and medium size datasets (≤ 128 tokens), either of the *RISK* methods could be chosen to fine-tune the model. This contrasts to the longer datasets where the hinge-loss modification has achieved the best results. In both cases, the results are in good agreement with those on the test sets.

Lastly, in Table 8, we further validate our use of the hinge-loss adaptation to the classical REINFORCE with baseline method – a staple in the reinforcement learning literature of language generation tasks (Paulus et al., 2018). Over the same three datasets of Table 7, we see that in the majority of instances the hinge-loss modification has been distinctively better than the standard approach. This confirms our intuition that the adoption of a hinge loss to restrict the gradient updates to "good" predictions only is beneficial to the improvement of ROUGE scores.

6 Conclusion

In this paper, we have proposed two variants to the reinforcement learning approaches typically used in sequence-to-sequence learning tasks. The two proposed approaches – nicknamed RwB-Hinge and RISK – have been designed to improve the reinforcement learning rewards by selecting and diversifying the predictions used during the fine-tuning of the model. In a set of automated summarisation experiments over nine, diverse datasets, the approaches have consistently led to improved performance, and also diversified the generated summaries. We note that, despite its commonplace use for summarisation evaluation, utilizing ROUGE as reinforcement learning reward does not easily translate into improved performance. For this reason, in the near future we plan to explore other contemporary score functions, such as BERTScore (Zhang et al., 2020b), in an attempt to build more effective rewards.

References

Kristjan Arumae and Fei Liu. 2018. Reinforced extractive summarization with question-focused rewards. In *Proceedings of ACL 2018, Student Research Workshop*, pages 105–111, Melbourne, Australia. Association for Computational Linguistics.

Sanghwan Bae, Taeuk Kim, Jihoon Kim, and Sanggoo Lee. 2019. Summary level training of sentence rewriting for abstractive summarization. In *Proceedings of the 2nd Workshop on New Frontiers in Summarization*, pages 10–20, Hong Kong, China. Association for Computational Linguistics.

Jacob Devlin, Ming-Wei Chang, Kenton Lee, and Kristina Toutanova. 2019. BERT: Pre-training of deep bidirectional transformers for language understanding. In *Proceedings of the 2019 Conference of the North American Chapter of the Association for Computational Linguistics: Human Language Technologies, Volume 1 (Long and Short Papers)*, pages 4171–4186, Minneapolis, Minnesota. Association for Computational Linguistics.

Rotem Dror, Gili Baumer, Segev Shlomov, and Roi Reichart. 2018. The hitchhiker's guide to testing statistical significance in natural language processing.

Sergey Edunov, Myle Ott, Michael Auli, David Grangier, and Marc'Aurelio Ranzato. 2018. Classical structured prediction losses for sequence to sequence learning. In *Proceedings of the 2018 Conference of the North American Chapter of the Association for Computational Linguistics: Human Language Technologies, Volume 1 (Long Papers)*, pages 355–364, New Orleans, Louisiana. Association for Computational Linguistics.

Alexander Fabbri, Irene Li, Tianwei She, Suyi Li, and Dragomir Radev. 2019. Multi-news: A large-scale multi-document summarization dataset and abstractive hierarchical model. In *Proceedings of the 57th Annual Meeting of the Association for Computational Linguistics*, pages 1074–1084, Florence, Italy. Association for Computational Linguistics.

Yang Gao, Wei Zhao, and Steffen Eger. 2020. SUPERT: Towards new frontiers in unsupervised evaluation metrics for multi-document summarization. In *Proceedings of the 58th Annual Meeting of the Association for Computational Linguistics*, pages 1347–1354, Online. Association for Computational Linguistics.

Max Grusky, Mor Naaman, and Yoav Artzi. 2018. Newsroom: A dataset of 1.3 million summaries with diverse extractive strategies. In *Proceedings of the 2018 Conference of the North American Chapter of the Association for Computational Linguistics: Human Language Technologies, Volume 1 (Long Papers)*, pages 708–719, New Orleans, Louisiana. Association for Computational Linguistics.

Ari Holtzman, Jan Buys, Li Du, Maxwell Forbes, and Yejin Choi. 2020. The curious case of neural text degeneration. In *International Conference on Learning Representations*.

Eric Jang, Shixiang Gu, and Ben Poole. 2017. Categorical reparameterization with gumbel-softmax. In *International Conference on Learning Representations*.

Mike Lewis, Yinhan Liu, Naman Goyal, Marjan Ghazvininejad, Abdelrahman Mohamed, Omer Levy, Veselin Stoyanov, and Luke Zettlemoyer. 2020. BART: Denoising sequence-to-sequence pre-training for natural language generation, translation, and comprehension. In *Proceedings of the 58th Annual Meeting of the Association for Computational Linguistics*, pages 7871–7880, Online. Association for Computational Linguistics.

Jiwei Li and Dan Jurafsky. 2016. Mutual information and diverse decoding improve neural machine translation. *CoRR*, abs/1601.00372.

Jiwei Li, Will Monroe, and Dan Jurafsky. 2016. A simple, fast diverse decoding algorithm for neural generation. *CoRR*, abs/1611.08562.

Siyao Li, Deren Lei, Pengda Qin, and William Yang Wang. 2019. Deep reinforcement learning with distributional semantic rewards for abstractive summarization. In *Proceedings of the 2019 Conference on Empirical Methods in Natural Language Processing and the 9th International Joint Conference on Natural Language Processing (EMNLP-IJCNLP)*, pages 6038–6044, Hong Kong, China. Association for Computational Linguistics.

Chin-Yew Lin. 2004. ROUGE: A package for automatic evaluation of summaries. In *Text Summarization Branches Out*, pages 74–81, Barcelona, Spain. Association for Computational Linguistics.

Yang Liu and Mirella Lapata. 2019. Text summarization with pretrained encoders. In *Proceedings of the 2019 Conference on Empirical Methods in Natural Language Processing and the 9th International Joint Conference on Natural Language Processing (EMNLP-IJCNLP)*, pages 3730–3740, Hong Kong, China. Association for Computational Linguistics.

Shashi Narayan, Shay B. Cohen, and Mirella Lapata. 2018a. Don't give me the details, just the summary! topic-aware convolutional neural networks for extreme summarization. In *Proceedings of the 2018 Conference on Empirical Methods in Natural Language Processing*, pages 1797–1807, Brussels, Belgium. Association for Computational Linguistics.

Shashi Narayan, Shay B. Cohen, and Mirella Lapata. 2018b. Ranking sentences for extractive summarization with reinforcement learning. In *Proceedings of the 2018 Conference of the North American Chapter of the Association for Computational Linguistics: Human Language Technologies, Volume 1 (Long Papers)*, pages 1747–1759, New Orleans, Louisiana. Association for Computational Linguistics.

Jong Won Park. 2020. Continual bert: Continual learning for adaptive extractive summarization of covid-19 literature. In *Proceedings of the 2020 NLP-COVID Workshop at the Conference on Empirical Methods in Natural Language Processing (EMNLP)*.

Ramakanth Pasunuru and Mohit Bansal. 2018. Multi-reward reinforced summarization with saliency and entailment. In *Proceedings of the 2018 Conference of the North American Chapter of the Association for Computational Linguistics: Human Language Technologies, Volume 2 (Short Papers)*, pages 646–653, New Orleans, Louisiana. Association for Computational Linguistics.

Romain Paulus, Caiming Xiong, and Richard Socher. 2018. A deep reinforced model for abstractive summarization. In *International Conference on Learning Representations*.

Colin Raffel, Noam Shazeer, Adam Roberts, Katherine Lee, Sharan Narang, Michael Matena, Yanqi Zhou, Wei Li, and Peter J. Liu. 2020. Exploring the limits of transfer learning with a unified text-to-text transformer. *Journal of Machine Learning Research*, 21(140):1–67.

Marc'Aurelio Ranzato, Sumit Chopra, Michael Auli, and Wojciech Zaremba. 2016. Sequence level training with recurrent neural networks. In *4th International Conference on Learning Representations, ICLR 2016, San Juan, Puerto Rico, May 2-4, 2016, Conference Track Proceedings*.

S. J. Rennie, E. Marcheret, Y. Mroueh, J. Ross, and V. Goel. 2017. Self-critical sequence training for image captioning. In *2017 IEEE Conference on Computer Vision and Pattern Recognition (CVPR)*, pages 1179–1195.

Ronald J. Williams. 1992. Simple statistical gradient-following algorithms for connectionist reinforcement learning. *Mach. Learn.*, 8(3–4):229–256.

Jingqing Zhang, Yao Zhao, Mohammad Saleh, and Peter Liu. 2020a. PEGASUS: Pre-training with extracted gap-sentences for abstractive summarization. In *Proceedings of the 37th International Conference on Machine Learning*, volume 119 of *Proceedings of Machine Learning Research*, pages 11328–11339. PMLR.

Tianyi Zhang, Varsha Kishore, Felix Wu, Kilian Q. Weinberger, and Yoav Artzi. 2020b. Bertscore: Evaluating text generation with bert. In *International Conference on Learning Representations*.

Chenguang Zhu, Ziyi Yang, Robert Gmyr, Michael Zeng, and Xuedong Huang. 2020. Make lead bias in your favor: Zero-shot abstractive news summarization. In *International Conference on Learning Representations*.

A Validation Scores

To determine an appropriate γ term for our mixed loss implementation, we have run tests with different values over the validation set for each dataset. To determine the best value, we have utilised the standard REINFORCE (Williams, 1992) approach combined linearly with the negative log-likelihood. We have chosen to optimise REINFORCE here since, being a close relative, but not the same as the algorithms we have used during training, it may help to eschew overfitting. In the interest of time, we have utilised the validation scores of a single seed to determine the γ values.

For the few-shot implementation in Table A.1, we have fixed the number of examples to fine-tune on (1,000) and the number of training iterations (2,000) exactly as in the standard baseline approach defined in Section 4. For the full-data approach in Table A.3, we have utilised all the training data, but, again in the interest of time, we have capped the number of training iterations to either: a) the same training time as the exhausted NLL tests reported in Table B.2, or b) 10,000 training iterations if the NLL training time exceeded 15,000 training iterations.

Tables A.2 and A.4 show the best γ values from the validation runs for all datasets. For datasets where there was no clear winner in Tables A.1 and A.3, we have compromised over the best values (highlighted in blue).

Table A.1: Validation scores of the baseline PEGASUS model, fine-tuned on a 1000 training examples for 2000 training iterations (few-shot). Best scores are highlighted.

Dataset	0.1	0.3	0.5	0.7	0.9
AESLC	28.96/13.12/28.49	30.26/14.55/29.49	31.21/15.22/30.26	30.46/14.65/29.70	31.25/15.64/30.42
ArXiv	28.06/7.99/20.70	33.01/10.58/21.24	29.49/9.32/21.12	33.46/10.46/22.55	33.43/10.55/22.26
Billsum	41.61/28.08/34.65	40.37/28.07/34.17	40.16/28.19/34.27	39.56/28.11/34.16	42.64/29.36/35.73
CNN/DM	40.30/18.37/28.33	39.47/17.41/27.79	39.79/18.03/27.91	40.44/17.81/28.12	40.98/18.06/28.09
Gigaword	39.24/16.81/35.65	38.97/17.42/35.94	39.92/17.56/36.45	40.27/17.96/36.91	40.91/18.48/37.42
Newsroom	36.61/25.35/33.15	36.93/25.39/33.25	36.36/24.57/32.68	38.07/26.15/34.23	35.98/23.53/32.12
Pubmed	31.74/10.69/19.50	33.44/11.37/21.35	34.96/12.07/21.62	37.35/13.02/22.14	36.57/12.99/22.47
Reddit-TIFU	19.43/4.45/15.74	24.87/6.56/20.08	25.00/6.19/19.99	25.73/6.85/20.55	26.50/6.90/20.86
XSum	41.19/17.59/32.90	41.28/17.48/32.27	41.79/17.97/32.65	42.30/18.80/34.11	43.43/19.58/34.76

Table A.2: A summary of the corresponding gamma weights determined from the above few-shot validation tests.

AESLC	ArXiv	Billsum	CNN/DM	Gigaword	Newsroom	Pubmed	Reddit-TIFU	XSum
0.9	0.7	0.9	0.9	0.9	0.7	0.7	0.9	0.9

Table A.3: Validation scores of the baseline PEGASUS model, fine-tuned on all training examples provided with the dataset for as many training iterations as either; the NLL baseline tests in Section 4, or 10,000 training iterations for longer datasets (ArXiv, Billsum, Pubmed). Best scores are highlighted.

Dataset	0.1	0.3	0.5	0.7	0.9
AESLC	28.66/11.52/28.35	32.81/15.45/32.48	33.39/15.77/32.98	33.23/16.36/32.75	34.94/17.17/34.11
ArXiv	5.71/0.00/5.56	1.76/0.23/1.70	1.61/0.04/1.59	10.08/1.40/9.09	13.19/2.46/11.59
Billsum	6.50/1.50/6.45	9.85/4.51/9.42	15.50/6.31/13.04	32.78/17.36/25.92	38.98/22.84/30.62
CNN/DM	3.50/0.004/0.35	15.37/5.75/14.91	24.36/8.12/22.58	29.17/11.46/27.44	35.56/14.87/33.29
Gigaword	28.48/11.90/27.23	39.89/18.35/37.28	41.61/18.89/38.49	43.67/20.51/40.30	42.68/19.34/39.26
Newsroom	31.48/21.03/28.32	27.73/15.08/24.05	26.78/13.79/22.84	33.92/20.89/30.19	35.56/22.58/31.77
Pubmed	1.04/0.12/1.03	0.29/0.00/0.29	0.77/0.08/0.76	6.34/1.78/5.12	10.98/2.29/8.96
Reddit-TIFU	1.08/0.06/1.08	11.59/1.43/10.45	9.15/1.24/8.63	14.71/2.58/12.59	23.25/5.79/18.94
XSum	23.04/6.44/17.45	34.02/12.04/25.35	35.56/12.61/26.10	38.84/15.98/30.94	41.60/18.16/33.43

Table A.4: A summary of the corresponding gamma weights determined from the above full-data validation tests.

AESLC	ArXiv	Billsum	CNN/DM	Gigaword	Newsroom	Pubmed	Reddit-TIFU	XSum
0.9	0.9	0.9	0.9	0.7	0.9	0.9	0.9	0.9

B   Model Hyperparameters

In our experiments, we have utilised the same hyperparameters used in the original PEGASUS paper (Zhang et al., 2020a). The exception to this is our use of a smaller batch size, constrained by computational resources. As batch size we have used 1, which has resulted in a drop in performance compared to that of the original paper. However, our fine-tuning approach is ensured to converge through the use of a convergence criterion. This is defined by a validation run that evaluates the model every 1000 training iterations, and monitors the progression of the validation loss over the entire training run. A model is deemed 'converged' if its validation loss does not decrease over 3000 training iterations.

Table B.1: Model hyperparameters used in the few-shot experiments. All values except the fine-tuning steps are also used in the full-data approach.

Dataset	Learning Rate	Label Smoothing	Fine-Tuning Steps	Batch Size	Beam Size	Max Input Tokens	Max Target Tokens
AESLC	5e-4	0.1	2000	1	1	512	32
ArXiv	5e-4	0.1	2000	1	1	1024	256
Billsum	5e-4	0.1	2000	1	1	1024	256
CNN/DM	5e-4	0.1	2000	1	1	1024	128
Gigaword	5e-4	0.1	2000	1	1	128	32
Newsroom	5e-4	0.1	2000	1	1	512	128
Pubmed	5e-4	0.1	2000	1	1	1024	256
Reddit-TIFU	5e-4	0.1	2000	1	1	1024	128
XSum	5e-4	0.1	2000	1	1	512	64

Table B.2: Model fine-tuning steps used in the full-data experiments. The NLL and all fine-tuning tests (except the validation tests), were validated every 1000 training iterations on a separate validation set, with the validation loss monitored over the run. An early stopping criterion was in place to stop training if the validation loss had not declined in 3000 consecutive training iterations. All methods have been averaged over three seed runs, whereas for the validation run we report results from a single run.

Dataset	NLL	Validation	RwB-Hinge	RISK-2	RISK-3
AESLC	7k	7k	5k	5.3k	5.3k
ArXiv	43k	10k	7k	7k	7k
Billsum	44k	10k	5k	5k	4.6k
CNN/DM	12k	12k	6.6k	6.6k	7.6k
Gigaword	10k	10k	5.6k	6k	6k
Newsroom	10k	10k	6.3k	6.6k	6.3k
Pubmed	55k	10k	5.6k	6k	6k
Reddit-TIFU	10k	10k	7k	7k	6.5k
XSum	8k	8k	6k	5.3k	6k

SMBOP: Semi-autoregressive Bottom-up Semantic Parsing

Ohad Rubin
Tel Aviv University
ohadr@mail.tau.ac.il

Jonathan Berant
Tel Aviv University
Allen Institute for AI
joberant@cs.tau.ac.il

Abstract

The de-facto standard decoding method for semantic parsing in recent years has been to autoregressively decode the abstract syntax tree of the target program using a top-down depth-first traversal. In this work, we propose an alternative approach: a Semi-autoregressive Bottom-up Parser (SMBOP) that constructs at decoding step t the top-K sub-trees of height $\leq t$. Our parser enjoys several benefits compared to top-down autoregressive parsing. From an efficiency perspective, bottom-up parsing allows to decode all sub-trees of a certain height in parallel, leading to logarithmic runtime complexity rather than linear. From a modeling perspective, a bottom-up parser learns representations for meaningful semantic sub-programs at each step, rather than for semantically-vacuous partial trees. We apply SMBOP on SPIDER, a challenging zero-shot semantic parsing benchmark, and show that SMBOP leads to a 2.2x speed-up in decoding time and a $\sim$5x speed-up in training time, compared to a semantic parser that uses autoregressive decoding. SMBOP obtains 71.1 denotation accuracy on SPIDER, establishing a new state-of-the-art, and 69.5 exact match, comparable to the 69.6 exact match of the autoregressive RAT-SQL+GRAPPA.

1 Introduction

Semantic parsing, the task of mapping natural language utterances into programs (Zelle and Mooney, 1996; Zettlemoyer and Collins, 2005; Clarke et al.; Liang et al., 2011), has converged in recent years on a standard encoder-decoder architecture. Recently, meaningful advances emerged on the encoder side, including developments in Transformer-based architectures (Wang et al., 2020a) and new pretraining techniques (Yin et al., 2020; Herzig et al., 2020; Yu et al., 2020; Deng et al., 2020; Shi et al., 2021). Conversely, the decoder has remained roughly constant for years, where the abstract syntax tree of the target program is autoregressively decoded in a

top-down manner (Yin and Neubig, 2017; Krishnamurthy et al., 2017; Rabinovich et al., 2017).

Bottom-up decoding in semantic parsing has received little attention (Cheng et al., 2019; Odena et al., 2020). In this work, we propose a bottom-up semantic parser, and demonstrate that equipped with recent developments in Transformer-based (Vaswani et al., 2017) architectures, it offers several advantages. From an efficiency perspective, bottom-up parsing can naturally be done *semi-autoregressively*: at each decoding step t, the parser generates *in parallel* the top-K program sub-trees of depth $\leq t$ (akin to beam search). This leads to runtime complexity that is logarithmic in the tree size, rather than linear, contributing to the rocketing interest in efficient and greener artificial intelligence technologies (Schwartz et al., 2020). From a modeling perspective, neural bottom-up parsing provides learned representations for meaningful (and executable) sub-programs, which are sub-trees computed during the search procedure, in contrast to top-down parsing, where hidden states represent partial trees without clear semantics.

Figure 1 illustrates a single decoding step of our parser. Given a beam Z_t with $K = 4$ trees of height t (blue vectors), we use *cross-attention* to contextualize the trees with information from the input question (orange). Then, we score the *frontier*, that is, the set of all trees of height $t + 1$ that can be constructed using a grammar from the current beam, and the top-K trees are kept (purple). Last, a representation for each of the new K trees is generated and placed in the new beam Z_{t+1}. After T decoding steps, the parser returns the highest-scoring tree in Z_T that corresponds to a full program. Because we have gold trees at training time, the entire model is trained jointly using maximum likelihood.

We evaluate our model, SMBOP [1] [2] (SeMi-

---

[1] Originally published in NAACL 2021.
[2] Rhymes with 'MMMBop'.

Proceedings of the 5th Workshop on Structured Prediction for NLP, pages 12–21
August 1–6, 2021. ©2021 Association for Computational Linguistics

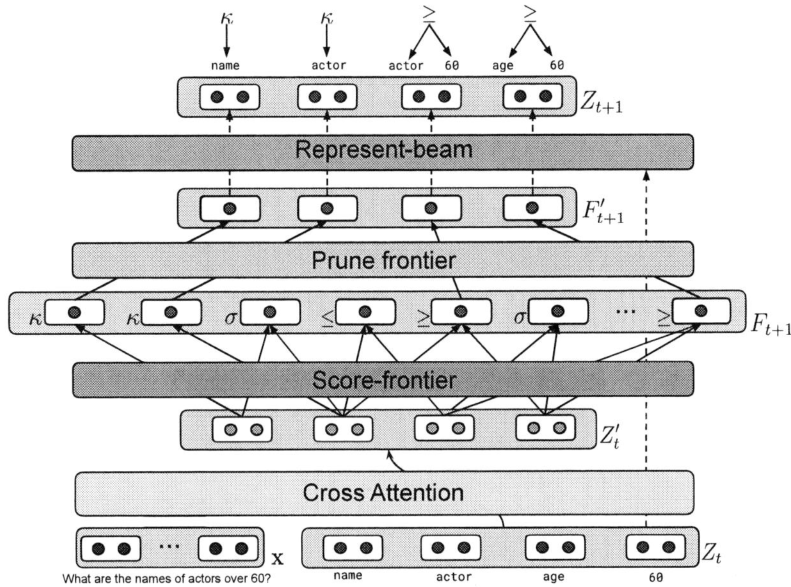

Figure 1: An overview of the decoding procedure of SMBOP. Z_t is is the beam at step t, Z'_t is the contextualized beam after cross-attention, F_{t+1} is the frontier ($\kappa, \sigma, \geq$ are logical operations applied on trees, as explained below), F'_{t+1} is the pruned frontier, and Z_{t+1} is the new beam. At the top we see the new trees created in this step. For $t = 0$ (depicted here), the beam contains the predicted schema constants and DB values.

autoregressive Bottom-up semantic Parser), on SPIDER (Yu et al., 2018), a challenging zero-shot text-to-SQL dataset. We implement the RAT-SQL+GRAPPA encoder (Yu et al., 2020), currently the best model on SPIDER, and replace the autoregressive decoder with the semi-autoregressive SM-BOP. SMBOP obtains an exact match accuracy of 69.5, comparable to the autoregressive RAT-SQL+GRAPPA at 69.6 exact match, and to current state-of-the-art at 69.8 exact match (Zhao et al., 2021), which applies additional pretraining. Moreover, SMBOP substantially improves state-of-the-art in denotation accuracy, improving performance from 68.3 → 71.1. Importantly, compared to autoregressive semantic parsing , we observe an average speed-up of 2.2x in decoding time, where for long SQL queries, speed-up is between 5x-6x, and a training speed-up of ∼5x.[3]

2 Background

Problem definition We focus in this work on text-to-SQL semantic parsing. Given a training set $\{(x^{(i)}, y^{(i)}, S^{(i)})\}_{i=1}^N$, where $x^{(i)}$ is an utterance, $y^{(i)}$ is its translation to a SQL query, and $S^{(i)}$ is the schema of the target database (DB), our goal is to

learn a model that maps new question-schema pairs (x, S) to the correct SQL query y. A DB schema S includes : (a) a set of tables, (b) a set of columns for each table, and (c) a set of foreign key-primary key column pairs describing relations between table columns. Schema tables and columns are termed schema constants, and denoted by $\mathcal{S}$.

RAT-SQL encoder This work is focused on decoding, and thus we implement the state-of-the-art RAT-SQL encoder (Wang et al., 2020b), on top of GRAPPA (Yu et al., 2020), a pre-trained encoder for semantic parsing. We now briefly review this encoder for completeness.

The RAT-SQL encoder is based on two main ideas. First, it provides a joint contextualized representation of the utterance and schema. Specifically, the utterance x is concatenated to a linearized form of the schema S, and they are passed through a stack of Transformer (Vaswani et al., 2017) layers. Then, tokens that correspond to a single schema constant are aggregated, which results in a final contextualized representation $(\mathbf{x}, \mathbf{s}) = (\mathbf{x}_1, \ldots, \mathbf{x}_{|x|}, \mathbf{s}_1, \ldots, \mathbf{s}_{|\mathbf{s}|})$, where $\mathbf{s}_i$ is a vector representing a single schema constant. This contextualization of x and S leads to better representation and alignment between the utterance and schema.

Second, RAT-SQL uses *relational-aware self-attention* (Shaw et al., 2018) to encode the structure of the schema and other prior knowledge on relations between encoded tokens. Specifically, given a sequence of token representations $(\mathbf{u}_1, \ldots, \mathbf{u}_{|\mathbf{u}|})$, relational-aware self-attention computes a scalar similarity score between pairs of token representations $e_{ij} \propto \mathbf{u}_i W_Q(\mathbf{u}_j W_K + \mathbf{r}_{ij}^K)$. This is identical to standard self-attention (W_Q and W_K are the query and key parameter matrices), except for the term $\mathbf{r}_{ij}^K$, which is an embedding that represents a relation between $\mathbf{u}_i$ and $\mathbf{u}_j$ from a closed set of possible relations. For example, if both tokens correspond to schema tables, an embedding will represent whether there is a primary-foreign key relation between the tables. If one of the tokens is an utterance word and another is a table column, a relation will denote if there is a string match between them. The same principle is also applied for representing the self-attention *values*, where another relation embedding matrix is used. We refer the reader to the RAT-SQL paper for details.

Overall, RAT-SQL jointly encodes the utterance, schema, the structure of the schema and alignments between the utterance and schema, and leads to state-of-the-art results in text-to-SQL parsing.

RAT-SQL layers are typically stacked on top of a pre-trained language model, such as BERT (Devlin et al., 2019). In this work, we use GRAPPA (Yu et al., 2020), a recent pre-trained model that has obtained state-of-the-art results in text-to-SQL parsing. GRAPPA is based on ROBERTA (Liu et al., 2019), but is further fine-tuned on synthetically generated utterance-query pairs using an objective for aligning the utterance and query.

Autoregressive top-down decoding The prevailing method for decoding in semantic parsing has been grammar-based autoregressive top-down decoding (Yin and Neubig, 2017; Krishnamurthy et al., 2017; Rabinovich et al., 2017), which guarantees decoding of syntactically valid programs. Specifically, the target program is represented as an abstract syntax tree under the grammar of the formal language, and linearized to a sequence of rules (or actions) using a top-down depth-first traversal. Once the program is represented as a sequence, it can be decoded using a standard sequence-to-sequence model with encoder attention (Dong and Lapata, 2016), often combined with beam search. We refer the reader to the aforementioned papers for further details on grammar-based decoding.

Algorithm 1: SMBOP

1 **input:** utterance x, schema S
2 $\mathbf{x}, \mathbf{s} \leftarrow \text{Encode}_{\text{RAT}}(x, S)$
3 $Z_0 \leftarrow$ Top-K schema constants and DB values
4 **for** $t \leftarrow 0 \ldots T - 1$ **do**
5 $\quad Z_t' \leftarrow \text{Attention}(Z_t, \mathbf{x}, \mathbf{x})$
6 $\quad F_{t+1} \leftarrow \text{Score-frontier}(Z_t')$
7 $\quad F_{t+1}' \leftarrow \arg\max_K(F_{t+1})$
8 $\quad Z_{t+1} \leftarrow \text{Represent-beam}(Z_t, F_{t+1}')$
9 **return** $\arg\max_z(Z_T)$

We now turn to describe our method, which provides a radically different approach for decoding in semantic parsing.

3 The SMBOP parser

We first provide a high-level overview of SMBOP (see Algorithm 1 and Figure 1). As explained in §2, we encode the utterance and schema with a RAT-SQL encoder. We initialize the beam (line 3) with the K highest scoring trees of height 0, which include either schema constants or DB values. All trees are scored independently and in parallel, in a procedure formally defined in §3.3.

Next, we start the search procedure. At every step t, attention is used to contextualize the trees with information from input question representation (line 5). This representation is used to score every tree on the *frontier*: the set of sub-trees of depth $\leq t + 1$ that can be constructed from sub-trees on the beam with depth $\leq t$ (lines 6-7). After choosing the top-K trees for step $t+1$, we compute a new representation for them (line 8). Finally, we return the top-scoring tree from the final decoding step, T. Steps in our model operate on tree representations independently, and thus each step is efficiently parallelized.

SMBOP resembles beam search as in each step it holds the top-K trees of a fixed height. It is also related to (pruned) chart parsing, since trees at step $t + 1$ are computed from trees that were found at step t. This is unlike sequence-to-sequence models where items on the beam are competing hypotheses without any interaction.

We now provide the details of our parser. First, we describe the formal language (§3.1), then we provide precise details of our model architecture (§3.2) including beam initialization (§3.3, we describe the training procedure (§3.4), and last, we discuss the properties of SMBOP compared to prior work (§3.5).

14

Operation	Notation	Input $\to$ Output
Set Union	$\cup$	$R \times R \to R$
Set Intersection	$\cap$	$R \times R \to R$
Set difference	$\setminus$	$R \times R \to R$
Selection	σ	$P \times R \to R$
Cartesian product	$\times$	$R \times R \to R$
Projection	Π	$C' \times R \to R$
And	$\wedge$	$P \times P \to P$
Or	$\vee$	$P \times P \to P$
Comparison	$\{\leq, \geq, =, \neq\}$	$C \times C \to P$
Constant Union	$\sqcup$	$C' \times C' \to C'$
Order by	$\tau_{asc/dsc}$	$C \times R \to R$
Group by	γ	$C \times R \to R$
Limit	λ	$C \times R \to R$
In/Not In	$\in, \notin$	$C \times R \to P$
Like/Not Like	$\sim, \nsim$	$C \times C \to P$
Aggregation	$\mathcal{G}_{\mathrm{agg}}$	$C \to C$
Distinct	δ	$C \to C$
Keep	κ	$\mathrm{Any} \to \mathrm{Any}$

Table 1: Our relational algebra grammar, along with the input and output semantic types of each operation. P: Predicate, R: Relation, C: schema constant or DB value, C': A set of constants/values, and $\mathrm{agg} \in \{\mathrm{sum}, \mathrm{max}, \mathrm{min}, \mathrm{count}, \mathrm{avg}\}$.

3.1 Representation of Query Trees

Relational algebra Guo et al. (2019) have shown recently that the mismatch between natural language and SQL leads to parsing difficulties. Therefore, they proposed SemQL, a formal query language with better alignment to natural language.

In this work, we follow their intuition, but instead of SemQL, we use the standard query language *relational algebra* (Codd, 1970). Relational algebra describes queries as trees, where leaves (terminals) are schema constants or DB values, and inner nodes (non-terminals) are operations (see Table 1). Similar to SemQL, its alignment with natural language is better than SQL. However, unlike SemQL, it is an existing query language, commonly used by SQL execution engines for query planning.

We write a grammar for relational algebra, augmented with SQL operators that are missing from relational algebra. We then implement a transpiler that converts SQL queries to relational algebra for parsing, and then back from relational algebra to SQL for evaluation. Table 1 shows the full grammar, including the input and output semantic types of all operations. A relation (R) is a tuple (or tuples), a predicate (P) is a Boolean condition (evaluating to `True` or `False`), a constant (C) is a schema constant or DB value, and (C') is a set of constants/values. Figure 2 shows an example re-

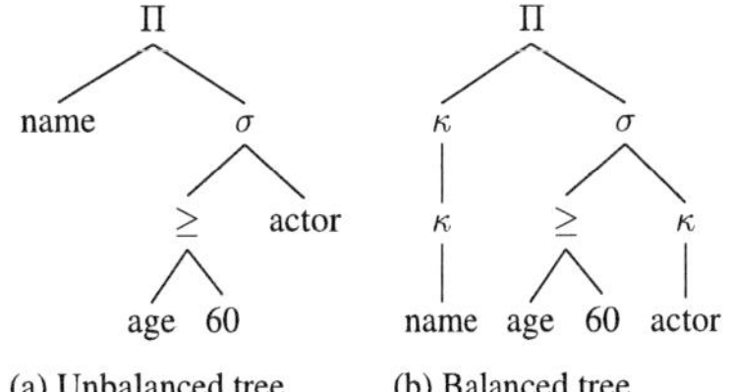

Figure 2: An unbalanced and balanced relational algebra tree (with the unary KEEP operation) for the utterance *"What are the names of actors older than 60?"*, where the corresponding SQL query is `SELECT name FROM actor WHERE age ≥ 60`.

lational algebra tree with the corresponding SQL query. More examples illustrating the correspondence between SQL and relational algebra (e.g., for the SQL `JOIN` operation) are in Appendix B. While our relational algebra grammar can also be adapted for standard top-down autoregressive parsing, we leave this endeavour for future work.

Tree balancing Conceptually, at each step SMBoP should generate new trees of height $\leq t + 1$ and keep the top-K trees computed so far. In practice, it is convenient to assume that trees are balanced. Thus, we want the beam at step t to only have trees that are of height exactly t (*t-high trees*).

To achieve this, we introduce a unary KEEP operation that does not change the semantics of the subtree it is applied on. Hence, we can always grow the height of trees in the beam without changing the formal query. For training (which we elaborate on in §3.4), we balance all relational algebra trees in the training set using the KEEP operation, such that the distance from the root to all leaves is equal. For example, in Figure 2, two KEEP operations are used to balance the column `actor.name`. After tree balancing, all constants and values are at height 0, and the goal of the parser at step t is to generate the gold set of t-high trees.

3.2 Model Architecture

To fully specify Alg. 1, we need to define the following components: (a) scoring of trees on the frontier (lines 5-6), (b) representation of trees (line 8), and (c) representing and scoring of constants and DB values during beam initialization (leaves). We now describe these components. Figure 3 illustrates the scoring and representation of a binary operation.

Scoring with contextualized beams SMBoP maintains at each decoding step a beam $Z_t =$

$((z_1^{(t)}, \mathbf{z}_1^{(t)}), \ldots, (z_K^{(t)}, \mathbf{z}_K^{(t)}))$, where $z_i^{(t)}$ is a symbolic representation of the query tree, and $\mathbf{z}_i^{(t)}$ is its corresponding vector representation. Unlike standard beam search, trees on our beams do not only compete with one another, but also *compose* with each other (similar to chart parsing). For example, in Fig. 1, the beam Z_0 contains the column age and the value 60, which compose using the $\geq$ operator to form the age $\geq$ 60 tree.

We contextualize tree representations on the beam using cross-attention. Specifically, we use standard attention (Vaswani et al., 2017) to give tree representations access to the input question: $Z'_t \leftarrow \text{Attention}(Z_t, \mathbf{x}, \mathbf{x})$, where the tree representations $(\mathbf{z}_1^{(t)}, \ldots, \mathbf{z}_K^{(t)})$ are the queries, and the input tokens $(\mathbf{x}_1, \ldots, \mathbf{x}_{|x|})$ are the keys and values.

Next, we compute scores for all $(t + 1)$-high trees on the frontier. Trees can be generated by applying either a unary (including KEEP) operation $u \in \mathcal{U}$ or binary operation $b \in \mathcal{B}$ on beam trees. Let $\mathbf{w}_u$ be a *scoring vector* for a unary operation (such as $\mathbf{w}_\kappa$, $\mathbf{w}_\delta$, etc.), let $\mathbf{w}_b$ be a *scoring vector* for a binary operation (such as $\mathbf{w}_\sigma$, $\mathbf{w}_\Pi$, etc.), and let $\mathbf{z}'_i, \mathbf{z}'_j$ be contextualized tree representations on the beam. We define a scoring function for frontier trees, where the score for a new tree z_{new} generated by applying a unary rule u on a tree z_i is defined as follows:

$$s(z_{\text{new}}) = \mathbf{w}_u^\top FF_U([\mathbf{z}_i; \mathbf{z}'_i]),$$

where FF_U is a 2-hidden layer feed-forward layer with relu activations, and $[\cdot; \cdot]$ denotes concatenation. Similarly the score for a tree generated by applying a binary rule b on the trees z_i, z_j is:

$$s(z_{\text{new}}) = \mathbf{w}_b^\top FF_B([\mathbf{z}_i; \mathbf{z}'_i; \mathbf{z}_j; \mathbf{z}'_j]),$$

where FF_B is another 2-hidden layer feed-forward layer with relu activations.

We use semantic types to detect invalid rule applications and fix their score to $s(z_{\text{new}}) = -\infty$. This guarantees that the trees SMBOP generates are well-formed, and the resulting SQL is executable. Overall, the total number of trees on the frontier is $\leq K|\mathcal{U}| + K^2|\mathcal{B}|$. Because scores of different trees on the frontier are independent, they are efficiently computed in parallel. Note that we score new trees from the frontier *before* creating a representation for them, which we describe next.

Recursive tree representation   after scoring the frontier, we generate a recursive vector representation for the top-K trees. While scoring is done with

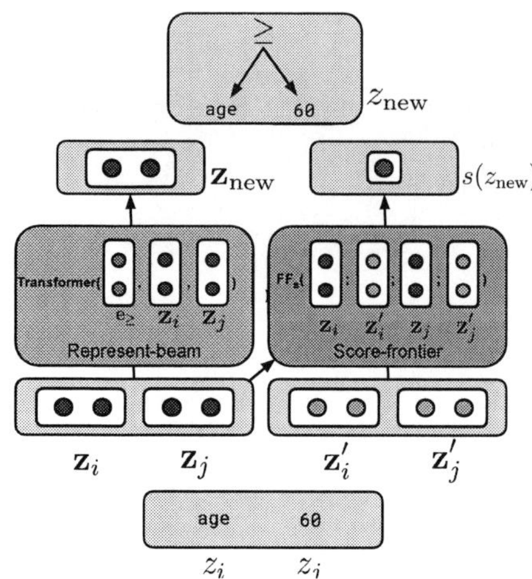

Figure 3: Illustration of our tree scoring and representation mechanisms. z is the symbolic tree, $\mathbf{z}$ is its vector representation, and $\mathbf{z}'$ its contextualized representation.

contextualized trees, representations are *not* contextualized. We empirically found that contextualized tree representations slightly reduce performance, possibly due to optimization issues.

We represent trees with another standard Transformer layer. Let $\mathbf{z}_{\text{new}}$ be the representation for a new tree, let e_ℓ be an embedding for a unary or binary operation, and let $\mathbf{z}_i, \mathbf{z}_j$ be non-contextualized tree representations from the beam we are extending. We compute a new representation as follows:

$$\mathbf{z}_{\text{new}} = \begin{cases} \text{Transformer}(\mathbf{e}_\ell, \mathbf{z}_i) & \text{unary } \ell \\ \text{Transformer}(\mathbf{e}_\ell, \mathbf{z}_i, \mathbf{z}_j) & \text{binary } \ell \\ \mathbf{z}_i & \ell = \text{KEEP} \end{cases}$$

where for the unary KEEP operation, we simply copy the representation from the previous step.

Return value   As mentioned, the parser returns the highest-scoring tree in Z_T. More precisely, we return the highest-scoring *returnable* tree, where a returnable tree is a tree that has a valid semantic type, that is, Relation (R).

3.3   Beam initialization

As described in Line 3 of Alg. 1, the beam Z_0 is initialized with K schema constants (e.g., actor, age) and DB values (e.g., 60, "France"). In particular, we independently score schema constants and choose the top-$\frac{K}{2}$, and similarly score DB values and choose the top-$\frac{K}{2}$, resulting in a total beam of size K.

Schema constants   We use a simple scoring function $f_{\text{const}}(\cdot)$. Recall that $\mathbf{s}_i$ is a representation of a constant, contextualized by the rest of the schema and the utterance. The function $f_{\text{const}}(\cdot)$ is a feed-forward network that scores each schema constant independently: $f_{\text{const}}(\mathbf{s}_i) = \mathbf{w}_{\text{const}} \tanh(W_{\text{const}}\mathbf{s}_i)$, and the top-$\frac{K}{2}$ constants are placed in Z_0.

DB values Because the number of values in the DB is potentially huge, we do not score all DB values. Instead, we learn to detect spans in the question that correspond to DB values. This leads to a setup that is similar to extractive question answering (Rajpurkar et al., 2016), where the model outputs a distribution over input spans, and thus we adopt the architecture commonly used in extractive question answering. Concretely, we compute the probability that a token is the start token of a DB value, $P_{\text{start}}(x_i) \propto \exp(\mathbf{w}_{\text{start}}^{\top}\mathbf{x}_i)$, and similarly the probability that a token is the end token of a DB value, $P_{\text{end}}(x_i) \propto \exp(\mathbf{w}_{\text{end}}^{\top}\mathbf{x}_i)$, where $\mathbf{w}_{\text{start}}$ and $\mathbf{w}_{\text{end}}$ are parameter vectors. We define the probability of a span $(x_i, \ldots, x_j)$ to be $P_{\text{start}}(x_i) \cdot P_{\text{end}}(x_j)$, and place in the beam Z_0 the top-$\frac{K}{2}$ input spans, where the representation of a span (x_i, x_j) is the average of $\mathbf{x}_i$ and $\mathbf{x}_j$.

A current limitation of SMBoP is that it cannot generate DB values that do not appear in the input question. This would require adding a mechanism such as "BRIDGE" proposed by Lin et al. (2020).

3.4   Training

To specify the loss function, we need to define the supervision signal. Recall that given the gold SQL program, we convert it into a gold *balanced relational algebra tree* z^{gold}, as explained in §3.1 and Figure 2. This lets us define for every decoding step the set of t-high gold sub-trees $\mathcal{Z}_t^{\text{gold}}$. For example $\mathcal{Z}_0^{\text{gold}}$ includes all gold schema constants and input spans that match a gold DB value,[4] $\mathcal{Z}_1^{\text{gold}}$ includes all 1-high gold trees, etc.

During training, we apply "bottom-up Teacher Forcing" (Williams and Zipser, 1989), that is, we populate[5] the beam Z_t with all trees from $\mathcal{Z}_t^{\text{gold}}$ and then fill the rest of the beam (of size K) with the top-scoring non-gold predicted trees. This guarantees that we will be able to compute a loss at each decoding step, as described below.

Loss function During search, our goal is to give high scores to the possibly multiple *sub-trees* of

---

[4]In Spider, in 98.2% of the training examples, all gold DB values appear as input spans.

[5]We compute this through an efficient tree hashing procedure. See Appendix A.

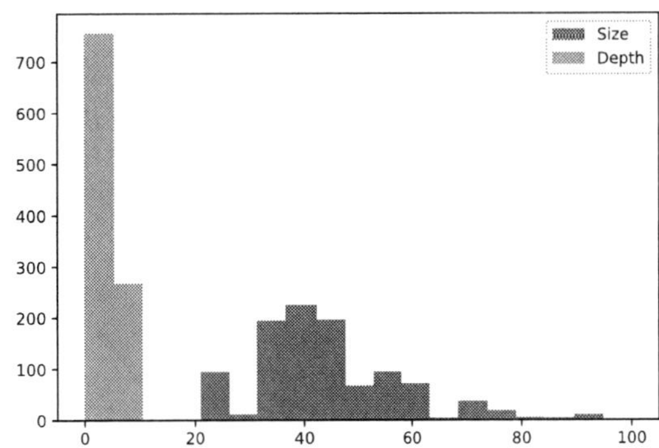

Figure 4: A histogram showing the distribution of the height of relational algebra trees in SPIDER, and the size of equivalent SQL query trees.

the gold tree. Because of teacher forcing, the frontier F_{t+1} is guaranteed to contain all gold trees $\mathcal{Z}_{t+1}^{\text{gold}}$. We first apply a softmax over all frontier trees $p(z_{\text{new}}) = \text{softmax}\{s(z_{\text{new}})\}_{z_{\text{new}} \in F_{t+1}}$ and then maximize the probabilities of gold trees:

$$\frac{1}{C} \sum_{t=0}^{T} \sum_{z_t \in \mathcal{Z}_t^{\text{gold}}} \log p(z_t)$$

where the loss is normalized by C, the total number of summed terms. In the initial beam, Z_0, the probability of an input span is the product of the start and end probabilities, as explained in §3.3.

3.5   Discussion

To our knowledge, this work is the first to present a semi-autoregressive bottom-up semantic parser. We discuss the benefits of our approach.

SMBoP has theoretical runtime complexity that is logarithmic in the size of the tree instead of linear for autoregressive models. Figure 4 shows the distribution over the height of relational algebra trees in SPIDER, and the size of equivalent SQL query trees. Clearly, the height of most trees is at most 10, while the size is 30-50, illustrating the potential of our approach. In §4, we demonstrate that indeed semi-autoregressive parsing leads to substantial empirical speed-up.

Unlike top-down autoregressive models, SM-BoP naturally computes representations $\mathbf{z}$ for all sub-trees constructed at decoding time, which are well-defined semantic objects. These representations can be used in setups such as *contextual semantic parsing*, where a semantic parser answers a sequence of questions. For example, given the questions *"How many students are living in the dorms?"* and then *"what are their last names?"*, the pronoun *"their"* refers to a sub-tree from the SQL tree of the first question. Having a representation for such sub-trees can be useful when parsing the second question, in benchmarks such as SPARC (Yu et al., 2019).

Another potential benefit of bottom-up parsing is that sub-queries can be executed while parsing (Berant et al., 2013; Liang et al., 2017), which can guide the search procedure. Recently, Odena et al. (2020) proposed such an approach for program synthesis, and showed that conditioning on the results of execution can improve performance. We do not explore this advantage of bottom-up parsing in this work, since executing queries at training time leads to a slow-down during training.

SMBOP is a bottom-up semi-autoregressive parser, but it could potentially be modified to be autoregressive by decoding one tree at a time. Past work (Cheng et al., 2019) has shown that the performance of bottom-up and top-down autoregressive parsers is similar, but it is possible to re-examine this given recent advances in neural architectures.

4 Experimental Evaluation

We conduct our experimental evaluation on SPIDER (Yu et al., 2018), a challenging large-scale dataset for text-to-SQL parsing. SPIDER has become a common benchmark for evaluating semantic parsers because it includes complex SQL queries and a realistic zero-shot setup, where schemas at test time are different from training time.

4.1 Experimental setup

We encode the input utterance x and the schema S with GRAPPA, consisting of 24 Transformer layers, followed by another 8 RAT-SQL layers, which we implement inside AllenNLP (Gardner et al., 2018). Our beam size is $K = 30$, and the number of decoding steps is $T = 9$ at inference time, which is the maximal tree depth on the development set. The transformer used for tree representations has one layer, 8 heads, and dimensionality 256. We train for 60K steps with batch size 60, and perform early stopping based on the development set.

Evaluation We evaluate performance with the official SPIDER evaluation script, which computes *exact match (EM)*, i.e., whether the predicted SQL query is identical to the gold query after some query normalization. The evaluation script uses

Model	EM	Exec
RAT-SQL+GP+GRAPPA	**69.8%**	n/a
RAT-SQL+GAP	69.7%	n/a
RAT-SQL+GRAPPA	69.6%	n/a
RAT-SQL+STRUG	68.4%	n/a
BRIDGE+BERT (ensemble)	67.5%	68.3
RAT-SQLv3+BERT	65.6%	n/a
SMBOP+GRAPPA	69.5%	**71.1%**

Table 2: Results on the SPIDER test set.

anonymized queries, where DB values are converted to a special `value` token. In addition, for models that output DB values, the evaluation script computes *denotation accuracy*, that is, whether executing the output SQL query results in the right denotation (answer). As SMBOP generates DB values, we evaluate using both EM and denotation accuracy

Models We compare SMBOP to the best non-anonymous models on the SPIDER leaderboard at the time of writing. Our model is most comparable to RAT-SQL+GRAPPA, which has the same encoder, but an autoregressive decoder.

In addition, we perform the following ablations and oracle experiments:

- NO X-ATTENTION: We remove the cross attention that computes Z_t' and uses the representations in Z_t directly to score the frontier. In this setup, the decoder only observes the input question through the 0-high trees in Z_0.

- WITH CNTX REP.: We use the contextualized representations not only for *scoring*, but also as input for creating the new trees Z_{t+1}. This tests if contextualized representations on the beam hurt or improve performance.

- NO DB VALUES: We anonymize all SQL queries by replacing DB values with `value`, as described above, and evaluate SMBOP using EM. This tests whether learning from DB values improves performance.

- Z_0-ORACLE: An oracle experiment where Z_0 is populated with the gold schema constants (but predicted DB values). This shows results given perfect schema matching.

4.2 Results

Table 2 shows test results of SMBOP compared to the top (non-anonymous) entries on the leaderboard (Zhao et al., 2021; Shi et al., 2021; Yu et al., 2020; Deng et al., 2020; Lin et al., 2020; Wang et al., 2020a). SMBOP obtains an EM of 69.5%, only

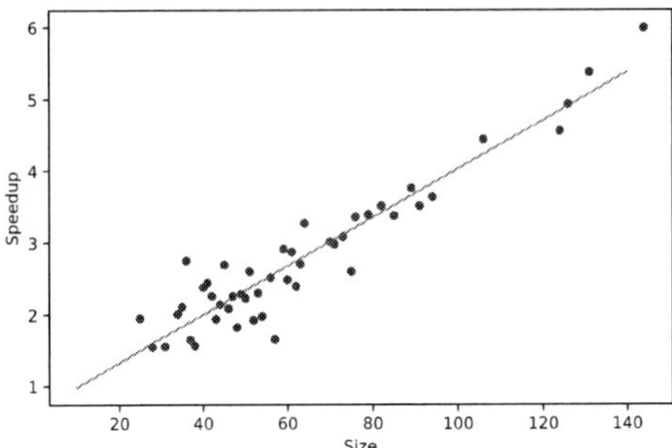

Figure 5: Speed-up on the development set compared to autoregressive decoding, w.r.t the size of the SQL query.

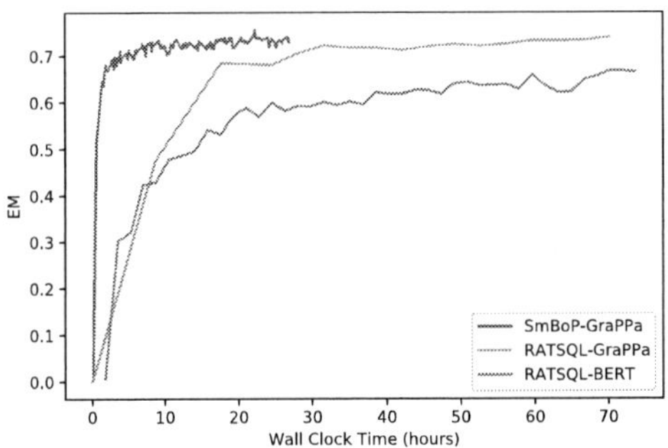

Figure 6: EM as a function of wall clock time on the development set of SPIDER during training.

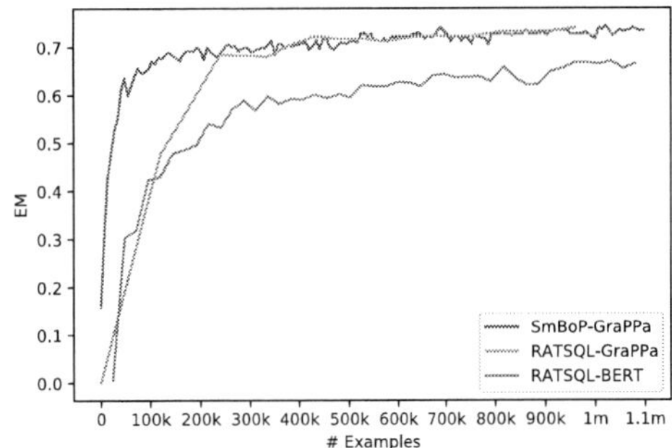

Figure 7: EM as a function of the number of examples on the development set of SPIDER during training.

0.3% lower than the best model, and 0.1% lower than RAT-SQL+GRAPPA, which has the same encoder, but an autoregressive decoder. Moreover, SMBOP outputs DB values, unlike other models that output anonymized queries that cannot be executed. SMBOP establishes a new state-of-the-art in denotation accuracy, surpassing an ensemble of BRIDGE+BERT models by 2.9 denotation accuracy points, and 2 EM points.

Turning to decoding time, we compare SMBOP to RAT-SQLv3+BERT, since the code for RAT-SQLv3+GRAPPA was not available. To the best of our knowledge the decoder in both is identical, so this should not affect decoding time. We find that the decoder of SMBOP is on average 2.23x faster than the autoregressive decoder on the development set. Figure 5 shows the average speed-up for different query tree sizes, where we observe a clear linear speed-up as a function of query size. For long queries the speed-up factor reaches 4x-6x. When including also the encoder, the average speed-up obtained by SMBOP is 1.55x.

In terms of training time, SMBOP leads to much faster training and convergence. We compare the learning curves of SMBOP and RAT-SQLv3+BERT, both trained on an RTX 3090, and also to RAT-SQLv3+GRAPPA using performance as a function of the number of examples, sent to us in a personal communication from the authors. SMBOP converges much faster than RAT-SQL (Fig. 7). E.g., after 120K examples, the EM of SMBOP is 67.5, while for RAT-SQL+GRAPPA it is 47.6. Moreover, SMBOP processes at training time 20.4 examples per second, compared to only 3.8 for the official RAT-SQL implementation. Combining these two facts leads to much faster training time (Fig. 6), slighly more than one day for SMBOP vs. 5-6 days for RAT-SQL.

5 Conclusions

In this work we present the first semi-autoregressive bottom-up semantic parser that enjoys logarithmic theoretical runtime, and show that it leads to a 2.2x speed-up in decoding and ∼5x faster taining, while maintaining state-of-the-art performance. Our work shows that bottom-up parsing, where the model learns representations for semantically meaningful sub-trees is a promising research direction, that can contribute in the future to setups such as contextual semantic parsing, where sub-trees often repeat, and can enjoy the benefits of execution at training time. Future work can also leverage work on learning tree representations (Shiv and Quirk, 2019) to further improve parser performance.

Acknowledgments

We thank Tao Yu, Ben Bogin, Jonathan Herzig, Inbar Oren, Elad Segal and Ankit Gupta for their useful comments. This research was partially supported by The Yandex Initiative for Machine Learning, and the European Research Council (ERC) under the European Union Horizons 2020 research and innovation programme (grant ERC DELPHI 802800).

References

J. Berant, A. Chou, R. Frostig, and P. Liang. 2013. Semantic parsing on Freebase from question-answer pairs. In *Empirical Methods in Natural Language Processing (EMNLP)*.

Jianpeng Cheng, Siva Reddy, Vijay Saraswat, and Mirella Lapata. 2019. Learning an executable neural semantic parser. *Computational Linguistics*, 45(1):59–94.

James Clarke, Dan Goldwasser, Ming-Wei Chang, and Dan Roth. Driving semantic parsing from the world's response. In *Proceedings of the Fourteenth Conference on Computational Natural Language Learning (CoNLL)*.

E. F. Codd. 1970. A relational model of data for large shared data banks. *Commun. ACM*, 13(6):377–387.

Xiang Deng, Ahmed Hassan Awadallah, Christopher Meek, Oleksandr Polozov, Huan Sun, and Matthew Richardson. 2020. Structure-grounded pretraining for text-to-sql. *arXiv preprint arXiv:2010.12773*.

Jacob Devlin, Ming-Wei Chang, Kenton Lee, and Kristina Toutanova. 2019. BERT: Pre-training of deep bidirectional transformers for language understanding. In *Proceedings of the 2019 Conference of the North American Chapter of the Association for Computational Linguistics: Human Language Technologies, Volume 1 (Long and Short Papers)*, pages 4171–4186, Minneapolis, Minnesota. Association for Computational Linguistics.

Li Dong and Mirella Lapata. 2016. Language to logical form with neural attention. In *Proceedings of the 54th Annual Meeting of the Association for Computational Linguistics (ACL)*, pages 33–43, Berlin, Germany. Association for Computational Linguistics.

Matt Gardner, Joel Grus, Mark Neumann, Oyvind Tafjord, Pradeep Dasigi, Nelson F. Liu, Matthew Peters, Michael Schmitz, and Luke Zettlemoyer. 2018. AllenNLP: A deep semantic natural language processing platform. In *Proceedings of Workshop for NLP Open Source Software (NLP-OSS)*, pages 1–6, Melbourne, Australia. Association for Computational Linguistics.

Jiaqi Guo, Zecheng Zhan, Yan Gao, Yan Xiao, Jian-Guang Lou, Ting Liu, and Dongmei Zhang. 2019. Towards complex text-to-SQL in cross-domain database with intermediate representation. In *Proceedings of the 57th Annual Meeting of the Association for Computational Linguistics (ACL)*,

pages 4524–4535, Florence, Italy. Association for Computational Linguistics.

Jonathan Herzig, Pawel Krzysztof Nowak, Thomas Müller, Francesco Piccinno, and Julian Eisenschlos. 2020. TaPas: Weakly supervised table parsing via pre-training. In *Proceedings of the 58th Annual Meeting of the Association for Computational Linguistics*, pages 4320–4333, Online. Association for Computational Linguistics.

Jayant Krishnamurthy, Pradeep Dasigi, and Matt Gardner. 2017. Neural semantic parsing with type constraints for semi-structured tables. In *Proceedings of the Conference on Empirical Methods in Natural Language Processing (EMNLP)*.

C. Liang, J. Berant, Q. Le, and K. D. F. N. Lao. 2017. Neural symbolic machines: Learning semantic parsers on Freebase with weak supervision. In *Association for Computational Linguistics (ACL)*.

Percy Liang, Michael Jordan, and Dan Klein. 2011. Learning dependency-based compositional semantics. In *Proceedings of the 49th Annual Meeting of the Association for Computational Linguistics: Human Language Technologies (ACL-HLT)*, pages 590–599, Portland, Oregon, USA. Association for Computational Linguistics.

Xi Victoria Lin, Richard Socher, and Caiming Xiong. 2020. Bridging textual and tabular data for cross-domain text-to-SQL semantic parsing. In *Findings of the Association for Computational Linguistics: EMNLP 2020*, pages 4870–4888, Online. Association for Computational Linguistics.

Yinhan Liu, Myle Ott, Naman Goyal, Jingfei Du, Mandar Joshi, Danqi Chen, Omer Levy, Mike Lewis, Luke Zettlemoyer, and Veselin Stoyanov. 2019. Roberta: A robustly optimized bert pretraining approach. *arXiv preprint arXiv:1907.11692*.

Ralph C. Merkle. 1987. A digital signature based on a conventional encryption function. In *Advances in Cryptology - CRYPTO '87, A Conference on the Theory and Applications of Cryptographic Techniques, Santa Barbara, California, USA, August 16-20, 1987, Proceedings*, volume 293 of *Lecture Notes in Computer Science*.

Augustus Odena, Kensen Shi, David Bieber, Rishabh Singh, and Charles Sutton. 2020. Bustle: Bottom-up program-synthesis through learning-guided exploration.

Maxim Rabinovich, Mitchell Stern, and Dan Klein. 2017. Abstract syntax networks for code generation and semantic parsing. In *Proceedings of the 55th Annual Meeting of the Association for Computational Linguistics (ACL)*, pages 1139–1149, Vancouver, Canada. Association for Computational Linguistics.

Pranav Rajpurkar, Jian Zhang, Konstantin Lopyrev, and Percy Liang. 2016. SQuAD: 100,000+ questions for machine comprehension of text. In *Proceedings of the 2016 Conference on Empirical Methods in Natural Language Processing*, pages 2383–2392, Austin, Texas. Association for Computational Linguistics.

Roy Schwartz, Jesse Dodge, Noah A. Smith, and Oren Etzioni. 2020. Green AI. *Communications of the ACM*, 63.

Peter Shaw, Jakob Uszkoreit, and Ashish Vaswani. 2018. Self-attention with relative position representations. In *Proceedings of the 2018 Conference of the North American Chapter of the Association for Computational Linguistics: Human Language Technologies (NAACL-HLT), Volume 2 (Short Papers)*, pages 464–468, New Orleans, Louisiana. Association for Computational Linguistics.

Peng Shi, Patrick Ng, Zhiguo Wang, Henghui Zhu, Alexander Hanbo Li, Jun Wang, Cicero Nogueira dos Santos, and Bing Xiang. 2021. Learning contextual representations for semantic parsing with generation-augmented pre-training. *arXiv preprint arXiv:2012.10309*.

Vighnesh Leonardo Shiv and Chris Quirk. 2019. Novel positional encodings to enable tree-structured transformers. In *Advances in Neural Information Processing Systems (NeurIPS)*.

Ashish Vaswani, Noam Shazeer, Niki Parmar, Jakob Uszkoreit, Llion Jones, Aidan N Gomez, Ł ukasz Kaiser, and Illia Polosukhin. 2017. Attention is all you need. In I. Guyon, U. V. Luxburg, S. Bengio, H. Wallach, R. Fergus, S. Vishwanathan, and R. Garnett, editors, *Advances in Neural Information Processing Systems (NeurIPS)*.

Bailin Wang, Richard Shin, Xiaodong Liu, Oleksandr Polozov, and Matthew Richardson. 2020a. RAT-SQL: Relation-aware schema encoding and linking for text-to-SQL parsers. In *Proceedings of the 58th Annual Meeting of the Association for Computational Linguistics (ACL)*.

Bailin Wang, Richard Shin, Xiaodong Liu, Oleksandr Polozov, and Matthew Richardson. 2020b. RAT-SQL: Relation-aware schema encoding and linking for text-to-SQL parsers. In *Proceedings of the 58th Annual Meeting of the Association for Computational Linguistics (ACL)*.

Ronald J. Williams and David Zipser. 1989. A learning algorithm for continually running fully recurrent neural networks. *Neural Computation*, 1(2):270–280.

Pengcheng Yin and Graham Neubig. 2017. A syntactic neural model for general-purpose code generation. In *Proceedings of the 55th Annual Meeting of the Association for Computational Linguistics (ACL)*, pages 440–450, Vancouver, Canada. Association for Computational Linguistics.

Pengcheng Yin, Graham Neubig, Wen-tau Yih, and Sebastian Riedel. 2020. TaBERT: Pretraining for joint understanding of textual and tabular data. In *Proceedings of the 58th Annual Meeting of the Association for Computational Linguistics*, pages 8413–8426, Online. Association for Computational Linguistics.

Tao Yu, Chien-Sheng Wu, Xi Victoria Lin, Bailin Wang, Yi Chern Tan, Xinyi Yang, Dragomir Radev, Richard Socher, and Caiming Xiong. 2020. Grappa: Grammar-augmented pre-training for table semantic parsing. *arXiv preprint arXiv:2009.13845*.

Tao Yu, Rui Zhang, Kai Yang, Michihiro Yasunaga, Dongxu Wang, Zifan Li, James Ma, Irene Li, Qingning Yao, Shanelle Roman, Zilin Zhang, and Dragomir Radev. 2018. Spider: A large-scale human-labeled dataset for complex and cross-domain semantic parsing and text-to-SQL task. In *Proceedings of the 2018 Conference on Empirical Methods in Natural Language Processing (EMNLP)*, pages 3911–3921, Brussels, Belgium. Association for Computational Linguistics.

Tao Yu, Rui Zhang, Michihiro Yasunaga, Yi Chern Tan, Xi Victoria Lin, Suyi Li, Irene Li Heyang Er, Bo Pang, Tao Chen, Emily Ji, Shreya Dixit, David Proctor, Sungrok Shim, Vincent Zhang Jonathan Kraft, Caiming Xiong, Richard Socher, and Dragomir Radev. 2019. Sparc: Cross-domain semantic parsing in context. In *Proceedings of the 57th Annual Meeting of the Association for Computational Linguistics (ACL)*, Florence, Italy. Association for Computational Linguistics.

John M. Zelle and Raymond J. Mooney. 1996. Learning to parse database queries using inductive logic programming. In *Proceedings of the Thirteenth National Conference on Artificial Intelligence (AAAI)*.

Luke S. Zettlemoyer and Michael Collins. 2005. Learning to map sentences to logical form: Structured classification with probabilistic categorial grammars. In *Proceedings of the Twenty-First Conference on Uncertainty in Artificial Intelligence (UAI)*.

Liang Zhao, Hexin Cao, and Yunsong Zhao. 2021. Gp: Context-free grammar pre-training for text-to-sql parsers.

Learning compositional structures for semantic graph parsing

Jonas Groschwitz
Saarland University
jonasg@coli.uni-saarland.de

Meaghan Fowlie
Utrecht University
m.fowlie@uu.nl

Alexander Koller
Saarland University
koller@coli.uni-saarland.de

Abstract

AM dependency parsing is a method for neural semantic graph parsing that exploits the principle of compositionality. While AM dependency parsers have been shown to be fast and accurate across several graphbanks, they require explicit annotations of the compositional tree structures for training. In the past, these were obtained using complex graphbank-specific heuristics written by experts. Here we show how they can instead be trained directly on the graphs with a neural latent-variable model, drastically reducing the amount and complexity of manual heuristics. We demonstrate that our model picks up on several linguistic phenomena on its own and achieves comparable accuracy to supervised training, greatly facilitating the use of AM dependency parsing for new sembanks.

1 Introduction

It is generally accepted in linguistic semantics that meaning is *compositional*, i.e. that the meaning representation for a sentence can be computed by evaluating a tree bottom-up. A compositional parsing model not only reflects this insight, but has practical advantages such as in compositional generalisation (e.g. Herzig and Berant 2020), i.e. systematically generalizing from limited data.

However, in developing a compositional semantic parser, one faces the task of figuring out what exactly the compositional structures – i.e. the trees that link the sentence and the meaning representation – should look like. This is challenging even for expert linguists; for instance, (Copestake et al., 2001) report that 90% of the development time of the English Resource Grammar (Copestake and Flickinger, 2000) went into the development of the syntax-semantics interface.

Compositional semantic parsers which are learned from data face an analogous problem: to train a such a parser, the compositional structures must be made explicit. However, these structures are not annotated in most sembanks. For instance, the *AM (Apply-Modify) dependency parser* of Groschwitz et al. (2018) uses a neural model to predict *AM dependency trees*, compositional structures that evaluate to semantic graphs. Their parser achieves high accuracy (Lindemann et al., 2019) and parsing speed (Lindemann et al., 2020) across a variety of English semantic graphbanks. To obtain an AM dependency tree for each graph in the corpus, they use hand-written graphbank-specific heuristics. These heuristics cost significant time and expert knowledge to create, limiting the ability of the AM parser to scale to new sembanks.

In this paper, we drastically reduce the need for hand-written heuristics for training the AM dependency parser. We first present a graphbank-independent method to compactly represent the relevant compositional structures of a graph in a tree automaton. We then train a neural AM dependency parser directly on these tree automata. Our code is available at github.com/coli-saar/am-parser.

We evaluate the consistency and usefulness of the learned compositional structures in two ways. We first evaluate the accuracy of the trained AM dependency parsers, across four graphbanks, and find that it is on par with an AM dependency parser that was trained on the hand-designed compositional structures of Lindemann et al. (2019). We then analyze the compositional structures which our algorithm produced, and find that they are linguistically consistent and meaningful. We expect that our methods will facilitate the design of compositional models of semantics in the future.

2 Related work

Compositional semantic graph parsers other than AM dependency parsers, like Artzi et al. (2015),

Proceedings of the 5th Workshop on Structured Prediction for NLP, pages 22–36
August 1–6, 2021. ©2021 Association for Computational Linguistics

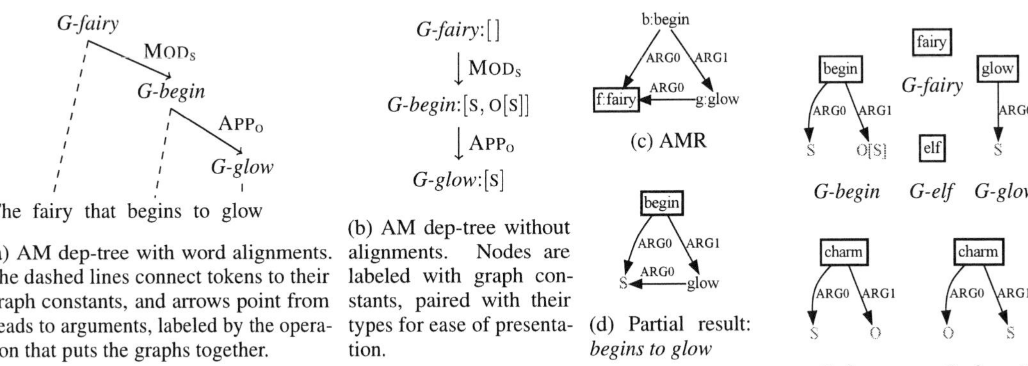

(a) AM dep-tree with word alignments. The dashed lines connect tokens to their graph constants, and arrows point from heads to arguments, labeled by the operation that puts the graphs together.

(b) AM dep-tree without alignments. Nodes are labeled with graph constants, paired with their types for ease of presentation.

(c) AMR

(d) Partial result: *begins to glow*

Figure 1: AM dep-trees and graphs for *the fairy that begins to glow*. We usually write our example AM dep-trees without alignments as in (b). We include node names where helpful, as in (c), where e.g. b is labeled *begin*.

Figure 2: Graph constants

Peng et al. (2015) and Chen et al. (2018), use CCG and HRG based grammars to parse AMR and EDS (Flickinger et al., 2017). They use a combination of heuristics, hand-annotated compositional structures and sampling to obtain training data for their parsers, in contrast to our joint neural technique. None of these approaches use slot names that carry meaning; to the best of our knowledge this work is the first to learn them from data.

Fancellu et al. (2019) use DAG grammars for compositional parsing of Discourse Representation Structures (DRS). Their algorithm for extracting the compositional structure of a graph is deterministic and graphbank-independent, but comes at a cost: for example, rules for heads require different versions depending on how often the head is modified, reducing the reusability of the rule.

Maillard et al. (2019) and Havrylov et al. (2019) learn compositional, continuous-space neural sentence encodings using latent tree structures. Their tasks are different: they learn to predict continuous-space embeddings; we learn to predict symbolic compositional structures. Similar observations hold for self-attention (Vaswani et al., 2017; Kitaev and Klein, 2018).

3 AM dependency parsing

Compositional semantic graph parsing methods do not predict a graph directly, but rather predict a compositional structure which in turn determines the graph. Groschwitz et al. (2018) represent the compositional structure of a graph with ***AM dependency trees*** (AM dep-trees for short) like the one in Fig. 1a. It describes the way the meanings of the words – the graph fragments in Fig. 2 – combine to form the semantic graph in Fig. 1c, here an AMR

(Banarescu et al., 2013). The AM dep-tree edges are labeled with graph-combining operations, taken from the *Apply-Modify (AM) algebra* (Groschwitz et al., 2017; Groschwitz, 2019).

Graphs are built out of fragments called ***graph constants*** (Fig. 2). Each graph constant has a ***root***, marked with a rectangular outline, and may have special node markers called ***sources*** (Courcelle and Engelfriet, 2012), drawn in red, which mark the empty slots where other graphs will be inserted.

In Fig. 1a, the APP$_O$ operation plugs the root of *G-glow* into the O source of *G-begin*. Because *G-begin* and *G-glow* both have an S-source, APP$_O$ merges these nodes, creating a ***reentrancy***, i.e. an undirected cycle, and yielding Fig. 1d, which is in turn attached at S to the root of *G-fairy* by MOD$_S$. APP fills a source of a head with an argument while MOD uses a source of a modifier to connect it to a head; both operations keep the root of the head.

Types The [S] annotation at the O-source of *G-begin* in Fig. 2 is a ***request*** as to what the ***type*** of the O argument of *G-begin* should be. The type of a graph is the set of its sources with their request annotations, so the request [S] means that the source set of the argument must be {S}. Because this is true of *G-glow*, the AM dependency tree is *well-typed*; otherwise the tree could not be evaluated to a graph. Thus, the graph constants lexically specify the semantic valency of each word as well as reentrancies due to e.g. control.

If a graph has no sources, we say it has the *empty type* [ ]; if a source in a graph printed here has no annotation, it is assumed to have the empty request (i.e. its argument must have no sources).

Parsing Groschwitz et al. (2018) use a neural supertagger and dependency parser to predict scores

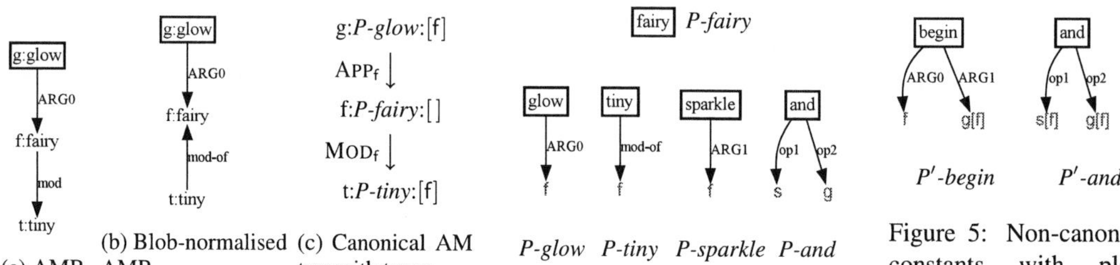

(a) AMR   (b) Blob-normalised AMR   (c) Canonical AM tree with types

Figure 3: *The tiny fairy glows.*

P-glow   P-tiny   P-sparkle   P-and

Figure 4: Canonical constants.

P′-begin   P′-and

Figure 5: Non-canonical constants with placeholder sources.

for graph constants and edges respectively. Computing the highest scoring well-typed AM dep-tree is NP-hard; we use their fixed-tree approximate decoder here.

4 Decomposition algorithm

The central challenge of compositional methods lies in the fact that the compositional structures are not provided in the graphbanks. Existing AM parsers (Groschwitz et al., 2018; Lindemann et al., 2019, 2020) use hand-built heuristics to extract AM dep-trees for supervised training from the graphs in the graphbank. These heuristics require extensive expert work, including graphbank-specific decisions for source allocations and graphbank- and phenomenon-specific patterns to extract type requests for reentrancies. In this section we present a simpler yet more complete method for obtaining the basic structure of an AM dep-tree for a given semantic graph G (for *decomposing* the graph), with much reduced reliance on heuristics. We will learn meaningful source names jointly with training the parser in §5 and §6.

Notation. We treat graphs as a quadruple $G = \langle N_G, r_G, E_G, L_G \rangle$, where the nodes N_G are arbitrary objects (in the examples here we use lowercase letters), $r_G \in N_G$ is the root, $E_G \subseteq N_G \times N_G$ is a set of directed edges, and L_G is the labelling function for the nodes and edges. For example in Fig. 3a, the node g is labeled "glow". The node identities are not relevant for graph identity or evaluation measures, but allow us to refer to specific nodes during decomposition. We formalize AM dep-trees as similar quadruples. Note that our example graphs are all AMRs, but our algorithms apply unchanged to all graphbanks

4.1 Basic transformation to AM dep-trees

Let us first consider the case where the semantic graph G has no reentrancies, like in Fig. 3a. The first step in obtaining the AM dep-tree for G is

to obtain the basic shape of the constants. We let each graph constant contain exactly one labeled node. Each edge belongs to the constant of exactly one node. The edges in the constant of a node are called its **blob** (Groschwitz et al., 2017); the blobs partition the edge set of the graph. For example, the blobs of the AMR in Fig. 3a are g plus the 'ARG0' edge, t plus the 'mod' edge, and f. We normalise edges so that they point away from the node to whose blob they belong, like in Fig. 3b, where the 'mod' edge is reversed and grouped with the node t to match *P-tiny* in Fig. 4. We add an *-of* suffix to the label of reversed edges. From here on, we assume all graph edges to be normalised this way.

Heuristics for this partition of edges into blobs are simple yet effective. Thus, this is the only part of this method where we still rely on graphbank-specific heuristics. (We use the same blob heuristics as Lindemann et al. (2019) in our experiments).

Once the decision of which edge goes in which blob is made, we obtain **canonical constants**, which are single node constants using **placeholder source names** and the empty request at every source; see e.g. *P-glow* in Fig. 4 (P for 'placeholder'). Placeholder source names are graph-specific source names: for a given argument slot in a constant, let n be the node that eventually fills it in G; we write n for the placeholder source in that slot. For example in the AM dep-tree in Fig. 3c the source f in *P-glow* (Fig. 4) gets filled by node f in the AMR in Fig. 3b. These placeholder sources are unique within the graph, allowing us to track source names through the AM dep-tree. When we restrict ourselves to the canonical constants, in a setting without reentrancies, the compositional structure is fully determined by the structure of the graph:

Lemma 4.1. *For a graph G without reentrancies, given a partition of G into blobs, there is exactly one AM dep-tree C_G with canonical constants that evaluates to G.*

We call this AM dep-tree the **canonical AM tree**

24

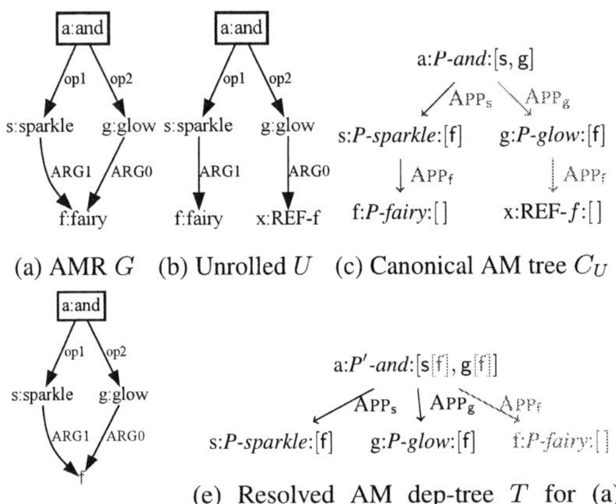

(a) AMR G (b) Unrolled U (c) Canonical AM tree C_U

(d) Partial result   (e) Resolved AM dep-tree T for (a); changes with respect to (c) in purple

Figure 6: Analysis for *The fairy sparkles and glows.*

$C_G = \langle N_G, r_G, E_C, L_C \rangle$ of G. Fig. 3c shows the canonical AM tree for the graph in Fig. 3b, using the canonical constants in Fig. 4. The canonical AM tree uses the same nodes and root as G, and essentially the same edges, but all edges point away from the root, forming a tree. Each node is labeled with its canonical constant. Each edge $n \rightarrow m \in E_C$ is labeled $\mathrm{APP_m}$ if the corresponding edge in the graph has the same direction, and is labeled $\mathrm{MOD_n}$ if there is instead an edge $m \rightarrow n$ in G.

4.2 Reentrancies and types

Finding AM dep-trees for graphs *with* reentrancies, like in Fig. 6a, is more challenging. To solve the problem in its generality, we first *unroll* the graph as in Fig. 6b, representing the reentrancy at f not directly, but with a *reference node* with label REF-f. Merging this REF-node with the node f it refers to yields the original graph again. (See §4.3 for our unrolling algorithm.) An unrolled graph U shares its non-REF-nodes with the original graph G. REF-nodes are always leaves.

We then obtain a canonical AM-tree C_U for the unrolled graph U as in §4.1 (see Fig. 6c), but REF-n nodes fill n-sources; e.g. x has an incoming APP_f edge here. C_U evaluates to U, not to G; we obtain an AM dep-tree that evaluates to G through a process called *resolving* the reentrancies, which removes all REF-nodes and instead expresses the reentrancies with the AM type system.

Fig. 6e shows the result T of applying this resolution process to C_U in Fig. 6c. In T, the s and g sources of the graph P'-*and* (see Fig. 5) each have a request [f] that signals that the f sources of *P-sparkle* and *P-glow* are still open when these graphs combine with P'-*and*, yielding the partial

---

Algorithm 1: Reentrancy resolution

1   $T \leftarrow$ the canonical AM-tree C_U of an unrolling U of G;

2   $R \leftarrow \{n \in N_G \mid \exists$ REF-n node in $U\}$;

3   **while** $R \neq \emptyset$:

4   Pick a $y \in R$ s.t. there is no $x \in R$, $x \neq y$, with y on an x-resolution path;

5   **for** $p \in y$-resolution paths:

6   **for** $n \xrightarrow{\mathrm{APP}} m \in p$:

7   **if** m is y or labeled REF-y:

8   Add $\beta(y)$ to the request at y in $\tau(n)$;

9   **else:**

10   Add y[$\beta(y)$] to the request at m in $\tau(n)$;

11   Move the subtree of T rooted at y up to be an APP_y daughter of RT (y), unless RT $(y) = y$;

12   Delete all REF-y nodes from T;

13    $R \leftarrow R - \{y\}$

14 **return** T

---

result in Fig. 6d. Since identical sources merge in the AM algebra, Fig. 6d has a single f-source slot. Into this slot, *P-fairy* is inserted to yield the original graph G in Fig. 6a, and we have obtained the reentrancy without using a REF-node. f is now a child of a in T; we call a the ***resolution target*** of f, RT (f). In general the resolution target of a node n is the lowest common ancestor of n and all nodes labeled REF-n.

Thus, to resolve the graph, we (a) add the necessary type requests to account for sources remaining open until they are merged at the resolution target and (b) make each node a dependent of its resolution target and remove all REF-nodes. Algorithm 1 describes this procedure. It uses the idea of an n-***resolution path***, which is a path between a node n or a REF-n node and its resolution target. In Fig. 6c, there are two f-resolution paths: one in blue between f and its resolution target a, and one in green between the REF-f node x and its resolution target a. Further, $\tau(n)$ is the type of the graph constant in T for a node n and $\beta(n)$ is the type of the result of evaluating the subtree below n in T.

In the example, Algorithm 1 iterates over all edges in both resolution paths (Line 6; the order of these iterations does not impact the result). For the two bottom edges $s \xrightarrow{\mathrm{APP}_f} f$ and $g \xrightarrow{\mathrm{APP}_f} x$, Line 8 applies. Since the subtree rooted at f evaluates to a constant with empty type, no actual changes are made here ($\beta(y)$ can be non-trivial from resolution paths handled previously). For the two upper edges $a \xrightarrow{\text{APP}_s} s$ and $a \xrightarrow{\text{APP}_g} g$, Line 10 applies, adding f to the requests at s and g in the constant at a. In Line 11, f gets moved up to become a child of its resolution target a and in Line 12 the REF-f node x gets removed, yielding T in Fig. 6e. Algorithm 1 is correct in the following precise sense:

Theorem 1. *Let G be a graph, let U be an unrolling of G, let C_U be the canonical AM-tree of U, and let T be the result of applying Algorithm 1 to C_U. Then T is a well-typed AM dep-tree that evaluates to G iff for all $y \in N_G$, for all y-resolution paths p in C,*

1. the bottom-most edge $n \to m$ of p (i.e. m is y or labeled REF-y) does not have a MOD label, and

2. for all y-resolution paths p in C, if $n \xrightarrow{\text{MOD}} m$ $\in p$, $n, m \neq y$, then there is a directed path in G from n to y.

Condition (1) captures the fact that moving MOD edges in the graph changes the evaluation result (the modifier would attach at a different node) and Condition (2) the fact that modifiers are not allowed to add sources to the type of the head they modify.

Algorithm 1 does not yield *all* possible AM dep-trees; in Appendix B, we present an algorithm that yields all possible AM dep-trees (with placeholder sources) for a graph. However, we find in practice that Algorithm 1 almost always finds the best linguistic analysis; i.e. reasons to deviate from Algorithm 1 are rare (we estimate that this affects about 1% of nodes and edges in the AM dep-tree). We leave handling these rare cases to future work.

4.3 Unrolling the graph

To obtain an unrolled graph U, we use Algorithm 2. The idea is to simply expand G through breadth-first search, creating REF-nodes when we encounter a node a second time. We use separate queues F and B for forward and backward traversal of edges, allowing us to avoid traversing edges backwards wherever possible, since that would yield MOD edges in the canonical AM-tree C_U, which can be problematic for the conditions of Theorem 1. And indeed, we can show that whenever there is an unrolled graph U satisfying the conditions of Theorem 1, Algorithm 2 returns one.

Algorithm 2 does not specify the order in which the incident edges of each node n are added to the

---

Algorithm 2: Unrolling

   Input: Graph G

1 $F, B \leftarrow$ empty FIFO queues;

2 $U \leftarrow$ empty graph;

3 add r_G to U, add outgoing edges of r_G to F and incoming edges of r_G to B;

4 **while** $F \cup B \neq \emptyset$:

5   **if** $F \neq \emptyset$: // `traverse forward`

6       $e \leftarrow F.$pop;

7       $n \leftarrow e.$target;

8   **else:** // `traverse backward`

9       $e \leftarrow B.$pop;

10      $n \leftarrow e.$origin;

11   Mark e as traversed;

12   **if** $n \notin N_U$:

13   add n, e to U;

14   add untraversed outgoing edges of n to F and incoming to B

15   **else:**

16   add new x to N_U; $L(x) = $ REF-n;

17   add e' to E_U where e' is just like e except with x in place of n

18 **return** U

---

queues, leaving an element of choice. However, we find that nearly all of these choices are unified later in the resolution process; meaningful choices are rare. For example in Fig. 6b, f and x may be switched, but Algorithm 1 always yields the AM dep-tree in Fig. 6e. In practice, we execute Algorithm 2 with arbitrary queueing order, and follow it with Algorithm 1. The AM dep-tree we obtain is guaranteed to be a decomposition of the original graph whenever one exists:

Theorem 2. *Let G be a graph partitioned into blobs. If there is a well-typed AM dep-tree T, using that blob partition, that evaluates to G, then Algorithm 2 (with any queueing order) and Algorithm 1 yield such a tree.*

5 Tree automata for source names

We have now seen how, for any graph G, we obtain a unique AM dependency tree T. This tree represents the compositional structure of G, but it still contains placeholder source names. We will now show how to automatically choose source names. These names should be consistent across the trees for different sentences; this yields reusable graph constants, which capture linguistic generalizations and permit more accurate parsing. But the source names must also remain consistent *within* each tree to ensure that the tree still evaluates correctly to G; for instance, if we replace the placeholder source f in *P-glow* in Fig. 6e by o, but we replace f in *P'-and* by s, then the AM dep-tree would not be well-typed because the request is not satisfied.

We therefore proceed in two steps. In this section, we represent all internally consistent source assignments compactly with a tree automaton. In §6, we then learn to select globally reusable source names jointly with training the neural parser.

Tree automata. A (bottom-up) tree automaton (Comon et al., 2007) is a device for compactly describing a language (set) of trees. It processes a tree bottom-up, starting at the leaves, and nondeterministically assigns states from a finite set to the nodes. A rule in a tree automaton has the general shape $f(q_1, \ldots, q_n) \to q$. If the automaton can assign the states $q_1, \ldots, q_n$ to the children of a node π with node label f, this rule allows it to assign the state q to π. The automaton *accepts* a tree if it can assign a *final state* to the root node. Tree automata can be seens as generalisation of parse charts.

General construction. Given an AM dependency tree T with placeholders, we construct a tree automaton that accepts all well-typed variants of T with consistent source assignments. More specifically, let $\mathcal{S}$ be a finite set of reusable source names; we will use $\mathcal{S} = \{s, o, m\}$ here, evoking subject, object, and modifier. The automaton will keep track of *source name assignments*, i.e. of partial functions ϕ from placeholder source names into $\mathcal{S}$. Its rules will ensure that the functions ϕ assign source names consistently.

We start by binarizing T into a binary tree B, whose leaves are the graph constants in T and whose internal nodes correspond to the edges of T; the binarized tree for the dependency tree in Fig. 7a is shown in Fig. 7b. We then construct a tree automaton A_B that accepts binarized trees which are isomorphic to B, but whose node labels have been replaced by graph constants and operations with reusable source names. The states of A_B are of the form $\langle \pi, \phi \rangle$, where ϕ is a source name assignment and π is the address of a node in B. Node addresses $\pi \in \mathbb{N}^*$ are defined recursively: the root has the empty address ϵ, and the i-th child of a node at address π has address πi. The final states are all states with $\pi = \epsilon$, indicating that we have reached the root.

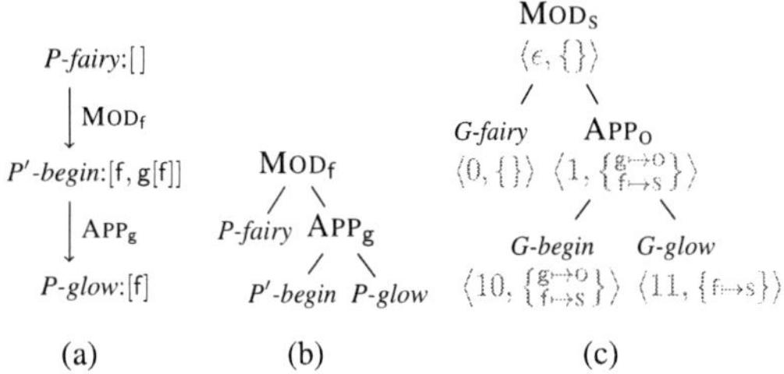

Figure 7: (a) AM dep-tree with placeholder sources for the graph in Fig. 1c, (b) its binarization B and (c) example automaton run (states in green).

Rules. The automaton A_B has two kinds of rules. *Leaf rules* choose injective source name assignments for constants; there is one rule for every possible assignment at each constant. That is, for every graph constant H at an address π in B, the automaton A_B contains all rules of the form

$$G \mapsto \langle \pi, \phi \rangle$$

where ϕ is an injective map from the placeholder sources in H to $\mathcal{S}$, and G is the graph constant identical to H except that each placeholder source s in H has been replaced by $\phi(s)$.

For example, the automaton for Fig. 7b contains the following rule:

$$G\text{-}begin \to \langle 00, \{g \mapsto o, f \mapsto s\} \rangle$$

Note that this rule uses the node label *G-begin* with the reusable source names, not the graph constant *P'-begin* in B with the placeholders.

In addition, *operation rules* percolate source assignments from children to parents. Let APP_x for some placeholder source x be the operation at address π in B. Then A_B contains all rules of the form

$$\text{APP}_{\phi_1(x)} (\langle \pi 0, \phi_1 \rangle, \langle \pi 1, \phi_2 \rangle) \to \langle \pi, \phi_1 \rangle$$

as long as ϕ_1 and ϕ_2 are identical where their domains overlap, i.e. they assign consistent source names to the placeholders. The rule passes ϕ_1 on to its parent. The assignments in ϕ_2 are either redundant, because of overlap with ϕ_1, or they are no longer relevant because they were filled by operations further below in the tree. The MOD case works out similarly.

In the example, A_B contains the rule

$$\text{APP}_o (\langle 10, \phi_b \rangle, \langle 11, \phi_g \rangle) \to \langle 1, \phi_b \rangle$$

where $\phi_b = \{g \mapsto o, f \mapsto s\}$ and $\phi_g = \{f \mapsto s\}$, because ϕ_b and ϕ_g agree on f. A complete accepting run of the automaton is shown in Fig. 7c.

The automaton A_B thus constructed accepts the binarizations of all well-typed AM dependency trees with sources in $\mathcal{S}$ that match T.

6 Joint learning of compositional structure and parser

As a final step, we train the neural parser of Groschwitz et al. (2018) directly on the tree automata. For each position i in the sentence, the parser predicts a score $c(G, i)$ for each graph constant G, and for each pair i, j of positions and operation ℓ, it predicts an edge score $c\left(i \xrightarrow{\ell} j\right)$.

The tree automata are factored the same way, in that they have one rule per graph constant and per dependency edge. As a result, we get a one-to-one correspondence between parser scores and automaton rules when aligning automata rules to words via the words' alignments to graph nodes.

We thus take the neural parser scores as *rule weights* $c(r)$ for rules r in the automaton. In a weighted tree automaton, the weight of a tree is defined as the product of the weights of all rules that built it. The *inside score* I of the tree automaton is the sum of the weights of all the trees it accepts. Computing this sum naively would be intractable, but the inside score can be computed efficiently with dynamic programming. Our training objective is to maximize the sum of the log inside scores of all automata in the corpus.

The arithmetic structure of computing the inside scores is complex and varies from automaton to automaton, which would make batching difficult. We solve this with the chain rule as follows:

$$\nabla_\theta \log I = \frac{1}{I} \nabla I = \frac{1}{I} \sum_{r \in A} \frac{\partial}{\partial c(r)} I \; \nabla_\theta c(r)$$

$$= \frac{1}{I} \sum_{r \in A} \alpha(r) \nabla_\theta c(r),$$

where θ are the parameters of the neural parser, which determine $c(r)$, and $\alpha(r)$ is the *outer weight* of the rule r (Eisner, 2016), i.e. the total weight of trees that use r divided by $c(r)$. The outer weight can be effectively computed with the inside-outside algorithm (Baker, 1979). This occurs outside of the gradient, so we do not need to backpropagate into it. Since the scores $c(r)$ are direct outputs of the neural parser, their gradients can be batched straightforwardly.

Method	DM	PAS	PSD	AMR
random trees	81.1	79.0	67.8	70.8
random weights	93.0	94.4	80.0	75.0
EM weights	93.8	94.3	81.7	75.2
joint neural model (§6)	**94.5**	**94.8**	**82.7**	**76.5**

Table 1: Baseline comparisons on the development sets (3 source names in all experiments).

7 Evaluation

7.1 Setup

We evaluate parsing accuracy on the graphbanks DM, PAS, and PSD from the SemEval 2015 shared task on Semantic Dependency Parsing (SDP, Oepen et al. (2015)) and on the AMRBank LDC2017T10 (Banarescu et al., 2013). We follow Lindemann et al. (2019) in the choice of neural architecture, in particular using BERT (Devlin et al., 2019) embeddings, and in the choice of decoder, hyperparameters and pre- and postprocessing (we train the model of §6 for 100 instead of 40 epochs, since it is slower to converge than supervised training). When a graph G is *non-decomposable* using our blob partition, i.e. if there is no well-typed AM dep-tree T that evaluates to G, and so the condition of Theorem 2 does not hold, then we remove that graph from the training set. (This does not affect coverage at evaluation time.) This occurs rarely, affecting e.g. about 1.6% of graphs in the PSD training set.

Like (Lindemann et al., 2019), we use the heuristic AMR alignments of (Groschwitz et al., 2018). These alignments can yield multi-node constants. In those cases, we first run the algorithm of Section 4 to obtain an AM tree with placeholder source names, and then consolidate those constants that are aligned to the same word into one constant, effectively collapsing segments of the AM tree into a single constant. We then construct the tree automata of Section 5 as normal.

7.2 Results

We consider three baselines. Each of these chooses a single tree for each training instance from the tree automata and performs supervised training. The **random trees** baseline samples a tree for each sentence from its automaton, uniformly at random. In the **random weights** baseline, we fix a random weight for each graph constant and edge label, globally across the corpus, and select the highest-scoring tree for each sentence. The **EM weights** baseline instead optimizes these global weights with the inside-outside algorithm.

| | DM | | PAS | | PSD | | AMR 17 |
	id F	ood F	id F	ood F	id F	ood F	Smatch F
He and Choi (2020)	94.6	90.8	96.1	94.4	86.8	79.5	-
FG'20	94.4	91.0	95.1	93.4	82.6	82.0	-
Bevilacqua et al. (2021)	-	-	-	-	-	-	84.5
L'19, w/o MTL	$93.9_{\pm0.1}$	$90.3_{\pm0.1}$	$94.5_{\pm0.1}$	$92.5_{\pm0.1}$	$82.0_{\pm0.1}$	$81.5_{\pm0.3}$	$76.3_{\pm0.2}$
This work	$94.2_{\pm0.0}$	$90.2_{\pm0.1}$	$94.6_{\pm0.0}$	$92.7_{\pm0.1}$	$81.4_{\pm0.1}$ $(75.8_{\pm0.1})$	$80.7_{\pm0.4}$ $(74.1_{\pm0.1})$	$75.1_{\pm0.2}$ $(74.2_{\pm0.3})$

Table 2: Semantic parsing accuracies (id = in domain test set; ood = out of domain test set). Results for our work are averages of three runs with standard deviations. L'19 are results of Lindemann et al. (2019) with fixed tree decoder (incl. post-processing bugfix for AMR as per Lindemann et al. (2020)). FG'20 is Fernández-González and Gómez-Rodríguez (2020).

Table 1 compares the baselines and the joint neural method. Random trees perform worst – consistency across the corpus matters. The difference between random weights and EM is suprisingly small, despite the EM algorithm converging well. The joint neural learning outperforms the baselines on all graphbanks; we analyze this in § 8. We also experimented with different numbers of sources, finding 3 to work best for DM, PAS and AMR, and 4 for PSD (all results in Appendix C).

Table 2 compares the accuracy of our joint model to Lindemann et al. (2019) and to the state of the art on the respective graphbanks. Our model is competitive with the state of the art on most graphbanks. In particular, our parsing accuracy is on par with Lindemann et al. (2019), who perform supervised training with hand-crafted heuristics. This indicates that our model learns appropriate source names.

Grahbank-specific pre- and processing. The pre- and postprocessing steps of (Lindemann et al., 2019) we use still rely on two graphbank-specific heuristics, that directly relate to AM depenency trees: in PSD, it includes a simple but effective step to make coordination structures more compatible with the specific flavor of application and modification of AM dependency trees. In AMR it includes a step to remove some edges related to coreference (a non-compositional source of reentrancy).

We include in brackets the results *without* those two preprocessing steps. The drop in performance for PSD indicates that while for the most part our method is graphbank-independent, not all shapes of graphs are equally suited for AM dependency-parsing and some preprocessing to bring the graph 'into shape' can still be important. For AMR, keeping the co-reference based edges leads to AM trees that resolve those reentrancies with the AM type system. That is, the algorithm 'invents' ad-hoc compositional explanations for a non-compositional phenomenon, yielding graph constants with type annotations that do not generalize well. The corresponding drop in performance indicates that extending AM dependency parsing to handle coreference will be an important future step when parsing AMR; some work in that direction has already been undertaken (Anikina et al., 2020).

8 Linguistic Analysis

As AM parsing is inherently interpretable, we can explore linguistic properties of the learned graph constants and trees. We find that the neural method makes use of both syntax and semantics.

We compute for each sentence in the training set the best tree from its tree automaton, according to the neural weights of the best performing epoch. We then sample trees from this set for hand-analysis (see Appendix A), to examine whether the model learned consistent sources for subjects and objects. We find that while the EM method uses highly consistent graph constants and AM operations, the neural method, which has access to the strings, sacrifices some graph constant and operation consistency in favour of *syntactic* consistency.

Syntactic Subjects and Objects. In the active sentence *The fairy charms the elf*, the phrase *the fairy* is the syntactic subject and *the elf* the syntactic object. In the passive *The elf is charmed (by the fairy)*, the phrase *the elf* is now the syntactic subject, even though in both sentences, the fairy is the charmer and the elf the charmee. Similarly, *the fairy* is the syntactic subject in the intransitive sentence *The fairy glows*.

Intra-Phenomenon Consistency. For both the EM and neural method, we found completely consistent source allocations for active transitive verbs in all four sembanks. These source allocations were also the overwhelming favourite graph constants for two-argument predicates (72-92%), and the most common sources used by Apply operations (94-98%). For example, in AMR, the graph constant template in Fig. 8a appears 26,653 times in the neural parser output. 74% of these used sources $x = $ S$_1$ and $y = $ S$_2$ (from $\mathcal{S} = \{$S$_1,$ S$_2,$ S$_3\}$). All active transitive sentences in our sample used this source allocation, so we call this the *active* graph constant (e.g. *G-charm* in Fig. 2) and refer to the sources S$_1$ and S$_2$ as S and O respectively, for *subject* and *object*. All four sembanks showed this kind of consistency; when we refer to S and O sources below, we mean whichever two sources displayed the same behaviour as S$_1$ and S$_2$ in AMR.

All four graphbanks are also highly consistent in their modifiers: classical modifiers such as adjectives are nearly universally adjoined with one consistent source – we refer to it as M – and MOD$_M$ is the overwhelming favourite (90-99%) for MOD operations.

Cross-Phenomenon Consistency. We call a parser *syntactically consistent* if its syntactic subjects fill the S slot, regardless of their semantic role. A syntactically consistent parser would acquire the AMR in Fig. 8c from the active sentence by the analysis in Fig. 8b, and from the passive sentence by the analysis in Fig. 8d, with the passive constant *G-charmP* from Fig. 2.

The neural parser is syntactically consistent: in all sembanks, it uses the same source S for syntactic subjects in passives as for actives. EM, conversely, prefers to use the same graph constants for active and passives, flipping the APP edges to produce syntactically inconsistent trees as in Fig. 8e. Single-argument predicates are also syntactically consistent in the neural model, using S for subjects and O for objects, while EM picks one source. The heuristics in Lindemann et al. (2019) have passive constants, but use them only when forced to, e.g. when coordinating active and passive.

Finally, we compute the entropy of the graph constants for the best trees of the training set as $\sum_G f(g) \ln f(G)$, where $f(G)$ is the frequency of constant G in the trees. The entropies are between 2 and 3 nats, but are consistently lower for EM than the neural method, by 0.031 to 0.079 nats. Considering that the neural method achieves higher parsing accuracies, using the most common graph constants and edges possible evidently is not always optimal for performance. The syntactic regularities exploited by the neural method may contribute to its improved performance.

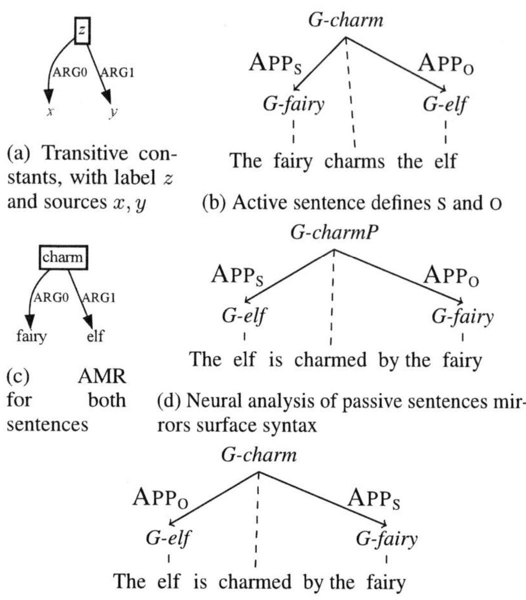

(a) Transitive constants, with label z and sources x, y

(b) Active sentence defines S and O

(c) AMR for both sentences

(d) Neural analysis of passive sentences mirrors surface syntax

(e) EM analysis of passives uses APP$_O$ for syntactic subject

Figure 8: AMR examples of active and passive. See Fig. 2 for graph constants.

9 Conclusion

In this work, we presented a method to obtain the compositional structures for AM dependency parsing that relies much less on graphbank-specific heuristics written by experts. Our neural model learns linguistically meaningful argument slot names, as shown by our manual evaluation; in this regard, our model learns to do the job of the linguist. High parsing performance across graphbanks shows that the learned compositional structures are also well-suited for practical applications, promising easier adaptation of AM dependency parsing to new graphbanks.

Acknowledgments

We would like to thank the anonymous reviewers as well as Lucia Donatelli, Pia Weißenhorn and Matthias Lindemann for their thoughtful comments. This research was in part funded by the Deutsche Forschungsgemeinschaft (DFG, German Research Foundation), project KO 2916/2-2, and by the Dutch Research Council (NWO) as part of the project *Learning Meaning from Structure* (VI.Veni.194.057).

References

Tatiana Anikina, Alexander Koller, and Michael Roth. 2020. Predicting coreference in Abstract Meaning Representations. In *Proceedings of the Third Workshop on Computational Models of Reference, Anaphora and Coreference*, pages 33–38, Barcelona, Spain (online). Association for Computational Linguistics.

Yoav Artzi, Kenton Lee, and Luke Zettlemoyer. 2015. Broad-coverage CCG Semantic Parsing with AMR. In *Proceedings of the 2015 Conference on Empirical Methods in Natural Language Processing*.

J. K. Baker. 1979. Trainable grammars for speech recognition. *The Journal of the Acoustical Society of America*, 65(S1):S132–S132.

Laura Banarescu, Claire Bonial, Shu Cai, Madalina Georgescu, Kira Griffitt, Ulf Hermjakob, Kevin Knight, Philipp Koehn, Martha Palmer, and Nathan Schneider. 2013. Abstract Meaning Representation for Sembanking. In *Proceedings of the 7th Linguistic Annotation Workshop and Interoperability with Discourse*.

Michele Bevilacqua, Rexhina Blloshmi, and Roberto Navigli. 2021. One SPRING to rule them both: Symmetric AMR semantic parsing and generation without a complex pipeline. In *Proceedings of AAAI*.

Yufei Chen, Weiwei Sun, and Xiaojun Wan. 2018. Accurate SHRG-based semantic parsing. In *Proceedings of the 56th Annual Meeting of the Association for Computational Linguistics (Volume 1: Long Papers)*, pages 408–418, Melbourne, Australia. Association for Computational Linguistics.

Hubert Comon, Max Dauchet, Rémi Gilleron, Florent Jacquemard, Denis Lugiez, Sophie Tison, Marc Tommasi, and Christof Löding. 2007. *Tree Automata techniques and applications*. published online - http://tata.gforge.inria.fr/.

Ann Copestake and Dan Flickinger. 2000. An open-source grammar development environment and broad-coverage english grammar using HPSG. In *Proceedings of the Second conference on Language Resources and Evaluation (LREC)*.

Ann Copestake, Alex Lascarides, and Dan Flickinger. 2001. An algebra for semantic construction in constraint-based grammars. In *Proceedings of the 39th ACL*.

Bruno Courcelle and Joost Engelfriet. 2012. *Graph Structure and Monadic Second-Order Logic, a Language Theoretic Approach*. Cambridge University Press.

Jacob Devlin, Ming-Wei Chang, Kenton Lee, and Kristina Toutanova. 2019. BERT: Pre-training of deep bidirectional transformers for language understanding. In *Proceedings of the 2019 Conference of the North American Chapter of the Association for Computational Linguistics: Human Language Technologies, Volume 1 (Long and Short Papers)*, pages 4171–4186, Minneapolis, Minnesota. Association for Computational Linguistics.

Jason Eisner. 2016. Inside-outside and forward-backward algorithms are just backprop (tutorial paper). In *Proceedings of the Workshop on Structured Prediction for NLP*, pages 1–17.

Federico Fancellu, Sorcha Gilroy, Adam Lopez, and Mirella Lapata. 2019. Semantic graph parsing with recurrent neural network DAG grammars. In *Proceedings of the 2019 Conference on Empirical Methods in Natural Language Processing and the 9th International Joint Conference on Natural Language Processing (EMNLP-IJCNLP)*, pages 2769–2778, Hong Kong, China. Association for Computational Linguistics.

Daniel Fernández-González and Carlos Gómez-Rodríguez. 2020. Transition-based semantic dependency parsing with pointer networks. In *Proceedings of the 58th Annual Meeting of the Association for Computational Linguistics*, pages 7035–7046, Online. Association for Computational Linguistics.

Dan Flickinger, Jan Hajič, Angelina Ivanova, Marco Kuhlmann, Yusuke Miyao, Stephan Oepen, and Daniel Zeman. 2017. Open SDP 1.2. LINDAT/CLARIN digital library at the Institute of Formal and Applied Linguistics (ÚFAL), Faculty of Mathematics and Physics, Charles University.

Jonas Groschwitz. 2019. *Methods for taking semantic graphs apart and putting them back together again*. Ph.D. thesis, Macquarie University and Saarland University.

Jonas Groschwitz, Meaghan Fowlie, Mark Johnson, and Alexander Koller. 2017. A constrained graph algebra for semantic parsing with AMRs. In *IWCS 2017 - 12th International Conference on Computational Semantics - Long papers*.

Jonas Groschwitz, Matthias Lindemann, Meaghan Fowlie, Mark Johnson, and Alexander Koller. 2018. AMR Dependency Parsing with a Typed Semantic Algebra. In *Proceedings of ACL*.

Serhii Havrylov, Germán Kruszewski, and Armand Joulin. 2019. Cooperative learning of disjoint syntax and semantics. In *Proceedings of the 2019 Conference of the North American Chapter of the Association for Computational Linguistics: Human Language Technologies, Volume 1 (Long and Short Papers)*, pages 1118–1128, Minneapolis, Minnesota. Association for Computational Linguistics.

Han He and Jinho Choi. 2020. Establishing strong baselines for the new decade: Sequence tagging, syntactic and semantic parsing with BERT. In *The Thirty-Third International Flairs Conference*.

Jonathan Herzig and Jonathan Berant. 2020. Span-based semantic parsing for compositional generalization.

Nikita Kitaev and Dan Klein. 2018. Constituency parsing with a self-attentive encoder. In *Proceedings of the 56th Annual Meeting of the Association for Computational Linguistics (Volume 1: Long Papers)*, pages 2676–2686, Melbourne, Australia. Association for Computational Linguistics.

Matthias Lindemann, Jonas Groschwitz, and Alexander Koller. 2019. Compositional semantic parsing across graphbanks. In *Proceedings of the 57th Annual Meeting of the Association for Computational Linguistics*, pages 4576–4585, Florence, Italy. Association for Computational Linguistics.

Matthias Lindemann, Jonas Groschwitz, and Alexander Koller. 2020. Fast semantic parsing with well-typedness guarantees. In *Proceedings of the 2020 Conference on Empirical Methods in Natural Language Processing (EMNLP)*, pages 3929–3951, Online. Association for Computational Linguistics.

Jean Maillard, Stephen Clark, and Dani Yogatama. 2019. Jointly learning sentence embeddings and syntax with unsupervised tree-LSTMs. *Natural Language Engineering*, 25(4).

Stephan Oepen, Marco Kuhlmann, Yusuke Miyao, Daniel Zeman, Silvie Cinková, Dan Flickinger, Jan Hajič, and Zdeňka Urešová. 2015. Semeval 2015 task 18: Broad-coverage semantic dependency parsing. In *Proceedings of the 9th International Workshop on Semantic Evaluation (SemEval 2015)*.

Xiaochang Peng, Linfeng Song, and Daniel Gildea. 2015. A synchronous hyperedge replacement grammar based approach for AMR parsing. In *Proceedings of the 19th Conference on Computational Language Learning*.

Ashish Vaswani, Noam Shazeer, Niki Parmar, Jakob Uszkoreit, Llion Jones, Aidan N. Gomez, undefine-dukasz Kaiser, and Illia Polosukhin. 2017. Attention is all you need. In *Proceedings of the 31st International Conference on Neural Information Processing Systems*, NIPS'17, page 6000–6010, Red Hook, NY, USA. Curran Associates Inc.

Learning compositional structures for semantic graph parsing
Supplementary Materials

Jonas Groschwitz
Saarland University
jonasg@coli.uni-saarland.de

Meaghan Fowlie
Utrecht University
m.fowlie@uu.nl

Alexander Koller
Saarland University
koller@coli.uni-saarland.de

A Sampling Method for hand analysis

To sample trees, we compute for each sentence in the training set the best tree from its tree automaton, according to the neural weights of the best performing epoch. This ensures the AM trees evaluate to the correct graph. We then sample trees from this set for hand-analysis.

To get relevant sentences, we sampled 5-to-15-word sentences with graph constants from the following six categories:

Transitive verbs: graph constants with a labeled root and two arguments with edges labelled as in Table 1:

Sembank	subject	object
AMR	ARG0	ARG1
DM	ARG1	ARG2
PAS	verb_ARG1	verb_ARG2
PSD	ACT_arg	PAT_arg

Table 1: Transitive verbs

As explained in the main text, we define the *active* constants as those with the most common source allocation, and the *passive* constants as those with the active source allocation flipped. We sampled both active and passive source allocations.

Verbs with one argument: Graph constants just like the transitive ones but lacking one of the arguments. There are four of these, given both source allocations.

Generally these graph constants are used for more than just verbs; for each of the six categories we sampled until we had ten relevant sentences. We visualised the AM trees and categorised the phenomena, for example active or passive verbs, nominalised verbs, imperatives, relative clauses, gerund modifiers, and so forth.

To answer the question of whether the parser used consistent constants for active and passive transitive sentences, we sampled until we had ten sentences with active or passive main verbs. For the single-argument verbs, we also looked at nominalised verbs, modifiers, and so forth. (Sampling and visualisation scripts will be available together with the rest of our code on GitHub.)

B An algorithm to obtain all AM dep-trees for a graph

Let G be a graph partitioned into blobs. Let $\mathcal{U}_G$ be the set of unrolled graphs for G that can be obtained by Algorithm 2 by varying the queue order.

Let further $\mathcal{M}_G$ be the set of results of Algorithm 3 below for every input AM dep-tree $T = C_U$ for $U \in \mathcal{U}_G$ and every choice of set M as specified in the algorithm. Algorithm 3 switches the order of two nodes m and k, making k the head of the subtree previously headed by m. This change of head is only possible when the incoming edge of m is labeled MOD (for APP, the change of head changes the evaluation result). It also requires a MOD edge between m and k; an APP edge with this type of swap would lead to a non-well-typed graph.

Finally, let $\mathcal{R}_G$ be the set of results of Algorithm 4 for every input AM dep-tree $T \in \mathcal{M}_G$ and any valid choice of R and RT (valid as described in the algorithm). Algorithm 4 is like Algorithm 1 for reentrancy resolution, but can have resolution targets RT (n) that are higher in the tree than the lowest common ancestor of n and the REF-n nodes. Further, Algorithm 4 uses the same methodology to also move nodes that do not need resolution to become descendents of a 'resolution target' higher in the tree (i.e. R here can now also contain nodes for which no REF node exists).

Then the following Theorem 1 holds:

# sources	DM	PAS	PSD	AMR
2	92.2	91.9	75.6	74.3
3	**94.5**	**94.8**	82.7	**76.5**
4	94.4	94.7	**83.4**	75.9
6	92.3	93.6	80.1	73.4

Table 2: Development set accuracies of the neural method for different numbers of source names.

C Additional Details

- AMR F-scores are *Smatch scores* (Cai and Knight, 2013)

- DM, PAS and PSD: We compute labeled F-score with the evaluation toolkit that was developed for the SDP shared task: `https://github.com/semantic-dependency-parsing/toolkit`

- We use the standard train/dev/test split for all corpora

- AMR corpus available through `https://amr.isi.edu/download.html` (requires LDC license)

- SDP corpora available through `https://catalog.ldc.upenn.edu/LDC2016T10` (requires LDC license)

Number of source names. We experimented with different numbers of source names in the joint neural method (Table 2). Mostly, three source names were most effective, except for PSD, where four were most effective. Two source names are not enough to model many common phenomena (e.g. ditransitive verbs, coordination of verbs); graphs containing these phenomena cannot be decomposed with two sources and are removed from the training set, reducing parsing accuracy. The higher performance of PSD with four sources may stem from PSD using flat coordination structures which require more source names; although this is also true for AMR where four source names are not beneficial. The drop with six source names may come from the fact that the latent space grows rapidly with more sources, making it harder to learn consistent source assignments.

Hyperparameters. See Table 3.

Algorithm 3: Modify-edge swapping

1 Input: an AM dep-tree T and a set M of pairs of consecutive edges in T of the form $\langle n \xrightarrow{\text{MoD}_n} m, m \xrightarrow{\text{MoD}_m} k \rangle$ such that no edge appears in multiple pairs.

2 **for** $\langle n \xrightarrow{\text{MoD}_n} m, m \xrightarrow{\text{MoD}_m} k \rangle \in M$**:**

3   Replace $n \xrightarrow{\text{MoD}_n} m$ in T with $n \xrightarrow{\text{MoD}_n} k$;

4   Replace $m \xrightarrow{\text{MoD}_m} k$ in T with $k \xrightarrow{\text{APP}_m} m$;

5   Add $\beta(m)$ (which always includes n) to the request at m in $\tau(k)$;

6 **return** T

Algorithm 4: Extended reentrancy resolution

1 Input: an AM dep-tree T; a set $R \supseteq \{n \in N_G \mid \exists \text{ REF-}n \text{ node in } T\}$; and a map RT that assigns to each node $n \in R$ a resolution target $\text{RT}(n)$, that is at least as high as the lowest common ancestor of n and all REF-n nodes (if they exist), and that satisfies the conditions of Theorem 1.

2 **while** $R \neq \emptyset$**:**

3   Pick a $y \in R$ s.t. there is no $x \in R$, $x \neq y$, with y on an x-resolution path;

4   **for** $p \in y$-*resolution paths***:**

5   **for** $n \xrightarrow{\text{APP}} m \in p$**:**

6   **if** m *is y or labeled REF-y***:**

7   Add $\beta(y)$ to the request at y in $\tau(n)$;

8   **else:**

9   Add y$[\beta(y)]$ to the request at m in $\tau(n)$;

10   Move the subtree of T rooted at y up to be an APP_y daughter of RT (y), unless $\text{RT}(y) = y$;

11   Delete all REF-y nodes from T;

12     $R \leftarrow R - \{y\}$

13 **return** T

Theorem 1. *Let G be a graph partitioned into blobs, and let $\mathcal{T}_G$ be the set of all well-typed AM dep-trees with placeholder sources, using that blob partition, that evaluate to G. Then if $\mathcal{T}_G = \emptyset$, all AM dep-trees in $\mathcal{R}_G$ are either not well-typed or do not evaluate to G. If however $\mathcal{T}_G \neq \emptyset$, then $\mathcal{R}_G = \mathcal{T}_G$.*

Activation function	tanh
Optimizer	Adam
Learning rate	0.001
Epochs	100
Dim of lemma embeddings	64
Dim of POS embeddings	32
Dim of NE embeddings	16
Minimum lemma frequency	7
Hidden layers in all MLPs	1
Hidden units in LSTM (per direction)	256
Hidden units in edge existence MLP	256
Hidden units in edge label MLP	256
Hidden units in supertagger MLP	1024
Hidden units in lexical label tagger MLP	1024
Layer dropout in LSTMs	0.3
Recurrent dropout in LSTMs	0.4
Input dropout	0.3
Dropout in edge existence MLP	0.0
Dropout in edge label MLP	0.0
Dropout in supertagger MLP	0.4
Dropout in lexical label tagger MLP	0.4

Table 3: Common hyperparameters used in all experiments (the random trees, random weights and EM weights baselines use 40 epochs since they converge faster). For a complete description of the neural architecture, see Lindemann et al. (2019) and its supplementary materials.

References

Shu Cai and Kevin Knight. 2013. Smatch: an evaluation metric for semantic feature structures. In *Proceedings of the 51st Annual Meeting of the Association for Computational Linguistics (Volume 2: Short Papers)*, pages 748–752, Sofia, Bulgaria. Association for Computational Linguistics.

Matthias Lindemann, Jonas Groschwitz, and Alexander Koller. 2019. Compositional semantic parsing across graphbanks. In *Proceedings of the 57th Annual Meeting of the Association for Computational Linguistics*, pages 4576–4585, Florence, Italy. Association for Computational Linguistics.

Offline Reinforcement Learning from Human Feedback in Real-World Sequence-to-Sequence Tasks

Julia Kreutzer[1]*, **Stefan Riezler**[2], **Carolin Lawrence**[3]

[1]Google Research, Montreal, Canada
[2]Computational Linguistics & IWR, Heidelberg University, Germany
[3]NEC Laboratories Europe, Heidelberg, Germany

jkreutzer@google.com,
riezler@cl.uni-heidelberg.de,
carolin.lawrence@neclab.eu

Abstract

Large volumes of interaction logs can be collected from NLP systems that are deployed in the real world. How can this wealth of information be leveraged? Using such interaction logs in an offline reinforcement learning (RL) setting is a promising approach. However, due to the nature of NLP tasks and the constraints of production systems, a series of challenges arise. We present a concise overview of these challenges and discuss possible solutions.

1 Introduction

When Natural Language Processing (NLP) systems are deployed in production, and interact with users ("the real world"), there are many potential ways of collecting feedback data or rich interaction logs. For example, one can ask for explicit user ratings (Kreutzer et al., 2018a), or collect user clicks (De Bona et al., 2010), or elicit user revisions (Trivedi et al., 2019) to get an estimate of how well the deployed system is doing. However, such user interaction logs are primarily used for an one-off assessment of the system, e.g., for spotting critical errors, detecting domain shifts, or identifying the most successful use cases of the system in production. This assessment can then be used to support the decision of keeping or replacing this system in production.

From a machine learning perspective, using interaction logs only for evaluation purposes is a lost opportunity for offline reinforcement learning (RL). Logs of user interactions are gold mines for off-policy learning, and they should be put to use, rather than being forgotten after a one-off evaluation purpose. To move towards the goal of using user interaction logs for learning, we will discuss

which challenges have hindered RL from being employed in real-world interaction with users of NLP systems so far.

Concretely, our focus is on sequence-to-sequence learning for NLP applications (see § 2 for an overview). For example, many machine translation services provide the option for users to give feedback on the quality of the translation, e.g., by collecting post-edits. Similarly, industrial chatbots can easily collect vast amounts of interaction logs, which can be utilized with offline RL methods (Kandasamy et al., 2017; Zhou et al., 2017; Hancock et al., 2019). In the following, we will thus present challenges that are encountered in user-interactive RL for NLP systems. With this discussion, we aim to (1) encourage NLP practitioners to leverage their interaction logs through offline RL, and (2) inspire RL researchers to steel their algorithms for the challenging applications in NLP.

2 Offline Feedback for Seq2Seq in NLP

In sequence-to-sequence (Seq2Seq) learning, the task is to map an input sequence $\mathbf{x} = x_1, x_2, \ldots, x_{|\mathbf{x}|}, \forall x_i \in \mathcal{X}$ to an output sequence $\mathbf{y} = y_1, y_2, \ldots, y_{|\mathbf{y}|}, \forall y_j \in \mathcal{Y}$, where $\mathcal{X}, \mathcal{Y}$ denote the sets of input and output vocabularies, respectively. The conditional distribution of the output sequence given the input can be modeled with a policy π_θ with learnable parameters θ. Assuming a left-to-right generation order, the output sequence $\mathbf{y}$ is generated by conditioning on previous output elements $\mathbf{y}_{<j}$ and the input sequence $\mathbf{x}$:

$$\pi_\theta(\mathbf{y} \mid \mathbf{x}) = \prod_{j=1}^{|\mathbf{y}|} \pi_\theta(y_j \mid \mathbf{y}_{<j}, \mathbf{x}). \quad (1)$$

Mapping the sequence-to-sequence problem formulation to NLP tasks, we have for example:

- Machine translation: $\mathbf{x}$ is a source sentence and $\mathbf{y}$ the translation of $\mathbf{x}$ in a target language.

---

*All authors contributed equally, order has been randomized (see https://bit.ly/38PgRjm).

Proceedings of the 5th Workshop on Structured Prediction for NLP, pages 37–43
August 1–6, 2021. ©2021 Association for Computational Linguistics

- Semantic parsing: $\mathbf{x}$ is a sentence and $\mathbf{y}$ its semantic parse (e.g., in SQL).
- Summarization: $\mathbf{x}$ is the document that is to be summarized and $\mathbf{y}$ a corresponding summary.
- Dialogue generation: $\mathbf{x}$ is the conversation history and $\mathbf{y}$ an appropriate reply.

The most distinctive feature of Seq2Seq NLP tasks for RL are the extremely large, structured output spaces: given the output vocabulary of size $|\mathcal{Y}|$ and a maximum sequence length M, there are $|\mathcal{Y}|^M$ possible combinations of output sequences. For instance, in machine translation there might be as many as $30\,000$ output tokens in the vocabulary and the output sequence length could easily be 100, leading to a total of $30\,000^{100}$ possible outputs.

A successful policy identifies the few combination of tokens that form valid output sequences. In the most extreme case only one output sequence exists that will be correct. , e.g., in a semantic parsing setup, where potentially only one specific SQL query will return the correct answer when executed. To train a policy, supervised data can be used. There we assume a given dataset $\mathcal{D}_{sup} = \{(\mathbf{x}_t, \mathbf{y}_t)\}_{t=1}^{T}$ on which the parameters θ can be learnt with a maximum likelihood approach, aiming to maximize the model score for the given reference output.

In practice, it may be too expensive to collect correct, i.e., supervised, output sequences, since they require skilled annotators, e.g., trained translators for a machine translation task. Therefore, one option is to pre-train the policy on some available supervised data, which will allow the model to concentrate on reasonable areas in the output space (Choshen et al., 2020). The model can then be used to produce potentially imperfect output sequences and humans can judge an output $\tilde{\mathbf{y}}$ and a reward $\delta_t \in [0, 1]$ is assigned. Model parameters may be optimized by pairing the model outputs with their reward estimates. Depending on the use case, quality judgments may also exist for single elements in the structure, adding $\delta_{(t,j)}$ for every step in the output sequence. The core idea is that the weighting by δ enables learning from imperfect outputs while respecting their faults. In RL, these quality assessments are used to reward desirable model actions, here desirable sequence outputs.

When collecting quality judgments from human users in production systems, it would be risky to directly update the model online according to their feedback.[1] Some user feedback might be adversarial, inappropriate, or not representative when used for training without prior treatment (Rivas et al., 2018; Kreutzer et al., 2018a; Davis, 2016).[2] Furthermore, interpreting feedback wrongly (e.g., through incorrect credit assignment (Bahdanau et al., 2017)), or receiving misleading feedback (Nguyen et al., 2017; Kreutzer et al., 2018a), could easily push the policy into less favorable conditions.

Because updating systems online is too risky, quality judgments are instead stored in interaction logs, i.e., $\mathcal{D}_{log} = \{(\mathbf{x}_t, \tilde{\mathbf{y}}_t, \delta_t)\}_{t=1}^{T}$, and the system is updated offline. As a result, the imperfect output sequences are produced by a possibly different policy, the logging policy μ, and updates to our learning policy are conducted offline, which is a classic *off-policy* RL scenario.

Due to the logging setup, the collected dataset is biased towards the choices of the deployed model, the logging policy μ. This results in a counterfactual learning scenario (Bottou et al., 2013). The bias may be corrected via importance sampling. If the logging policy is known and $\mu(\hat{\mathbf{y}} \mid \mathbf{x})$ is logged as well, the policy can then be optimized for the Inverse Propensity Scoring (IPS) objective (Rosenbaum and Rubin, 1983):

$$\mathcal{L}_{\text{IPS}} = -\frac{1}{T} \sum_{t=1}^{T} \delta_t \frac{\pi_\theta(\tilde{\mathbf{y}}_t \mid \mathbf{x}_t)}{\mu(\tilde{\mathbf{y}}_t \mid \mathbf{x}_t)}. \tag{2}$$

3 Challenges for Off-Policy RL in NLP

On top of the difficulties encountered in offline RL, additionally constraints arise in production scenarios. We address this and possible solutions in §3.1, while §3.2 focuses on how to obtain reliable data from which machine learning can succeed.

3.1 Deterministic Logging and Off-line Learning

In order to not show inferior outputs to users, production NLP systems show the most likely output, which disables the typically crucial exploration component of RL. This effectively results in deterministic logging policies that lack explicit exploration, which makes an application of standard off-

---

[1] The majority of RL research in NLP has focused on learning from online feedback (Sokolov et al., 2016; He et al., 2016; Li et al., 2016; Bahdanau et al., 2017; Nguyen et al., 2017; Nogueira and Cho, 2017; Lam et al., 2018).

[2] The chatbot Tay might be one of the most illustrative examples for what can go wrong (Davis, 2016).

policy methods for counterfactual learning questionable. For example, techniques such as inverse propensity scoring (Rosenbaum and Rubin, 1983) or weighted importance sampling (Precup et al., 2000; Jiang and Li, 2016; Thomas and Brunskill, 2016), rely on sufficient exploration of the output space by the logging system as a prerequisite for counterfactual learning. In fact, Langford et al. (2008) and Strehl et al. (2010) even give impossibility results for *exploration-free counterfactual learning*.

One option is to hope for *implicit exploration* due to input or context variability. This has been observed for the case of online advertising (Chapelle and Li, 2011) and investigated theoretically (Bastani et al., 2017). In NLP, output sequences may overlap in some of the words, so the learner could infer from rewards in which contexts specific words are more suitable than in others. This has been explored in the context of machine translation (Lawrence et al., 2017b), utilizing the Deterministic Propensity Matching (DPM) objective

$$\mathcal{L}_{\text{DPM}} = -\frac{1}{T} \sum_{t=1}^{T} \delta_t \pi_\theta(\tilde{\mathbf{y}}_t \mid \mathbf{x}_t), \qquad (3)$$

which closely follows the IPS objective, however, due to the deterministic logging $\forall \tilde{\mathbf{y}}, \mu(\tilde{\mathbf{y}} \mid \mathbf{x}) = 1$. While this exploration is limited by the input data, solutions for safe exploration might be attractive to transfer to NLP applications to actively guide exploration while not sacrificing quality (Hans et al., 2008; Berkenkamp et al., 2017).

Another option is to consider concrete cases of *degenerate behavior* in estimation from logged data. We look at two such issues and possible solutions. Both problems occur irrespective of whether data is logged deterministically or not, but the effects of the degenerative behavior might be amplified in the case of deterministic logging.

The first form of degenerate behaviour occurs for a collected log $\mathcal{D}_{log}$ with $\delta \in [0,1]$ because IPS and DPM can trivially be minimized by setting all probabilities in the dataset $\mathcal{D}$ to 1 for any $\delta_t > 0$ (Lawrence et al., 2017a). Concretely, this means, while the worst output sequences with $\delta_t = 0$ are simply ignored, all other sequences are encouraged, even if their reward is close to 0. However, it is clearly undesirable to increase the probability of low reward examples (Swaminathan and Joachims, 2015; Lawrence et al., 2017b,a).

There are two possible solutions to this problem:

The first solution is to tune the learning rate and perform early stopping before the degenerate state can be reached. The second solution is to utilize a *multiplicative control variate* (Kong, 1992) for self-normalization (Swaminathan and Joachims, 2015). For efficient gradient calculation, batches of size B can be reweighted one-step-late (OSL) (Lawrence and Riezler, 2018) using θ' from some previous iteration:

$$\mathcal{L}_{\text{OSL}} = -\frac{\frac{1}{B} \sum_{b=1}^{B} \delta_b \pi_\theta(\tilde{\mathbf{y}}_b \mid \mathbf{x}_b)}{\frac{1}{T} \sum_{t=1}^{T} \pi_{\theta'}(\tilde{\mathbf{y}}_t \mid \mathbf{x}_t)}. \qquad (4)$$

Self-normalization discourages increasing the probability of low reward data because this would take away probability mass from higher reward outputs and as a result. This introduces a bias in the estimator (that decreases as T increases), however, it makes learning under deterministic logging feasible, as has been shown for learning with real human feedback in a semantic parsing scenario (Lawrence and Riezler, 2018). This gives the RL agent an edge in learning in an environment that has been deemed impossible in the literature.

A second form of degenerate behavior occurs because the reward δ_t of an output sequence is typically measured with some non-negative value, e.g., $\delta_t \in [0,1]$. For example, for machine translation, Kreutzer et al. (2018b) collect ratings for translations on a 5-point Likert scale and map the values linearly to $[0,1]$. However, utilizing any of the above objectives means that bad output sequences with low rewards cannot actively be discouraged.

There are two possible solutions, both of which have been used as *additive control variates* to reduce variance in gradient estimators. First, low reward sequences can be discouraged by employing a reward baseline, where for example the average reward $\Delta = \frac{1}{t} \sum_{t'=1}^{t} \delta_{t'}$ is subtracted from each δ_t. This will cause output sequences worse than the running average to be discouraged rather than encouraged. The second option is to use the logged data $\mathcal{D}_{log}$ to learn a *reward estimator* $\hat{\delta}$ that can return a reward estimate for any pair $(\mathbf{x}, \mathbf{y})$. This estimator together with the IPS objective leads to the Doubly Robust (DR) objective (Dudik et al., 2011),

$$\mathcal{L}_{\mathrm{DR}} = -\frac{1}{T} \sum_{t=1}^{T} \Big[(\delta_t - \hat{\delta}(\mathbf{x}_t, \tilde{\mathbf{y}}_t)) \, \pi_\theta(\tilde{\mathbf{y}}_t \mid \mathbf{x}_t) +$$

$$\sum_{\tilde{\mathbf{y}}' \sim \pi_\theta(\tilde{\mathbf{y}} \mid \mathbf{x}_t)} \hat{\delta}(\mathbf{x}_t, \tilde{\mathbf{y}}') \, \pi_\theta(\tilde{\mathbf{y}}' \mid \mathbf{x}_t) \Big].$$

This objective enables the exploration of other outputs $\tilde{\mathbf{y}}'$ that are not part of the original log and encourages them based on the reward value returned by the estimator. For the task of machine translation, Lawrence et al. (2017b) show this objective to be the most successful in their setup, and Kreutzer et al. (2018a) report simulation results that show that this objective can significantly reduce the gap between offline and online policy learning, even if the reward estimator is not perfect. Zhou et al. (2017) present an alternating approach to integrating a reward estimator for exploration, by switching between learning offline from logged rewards and exploring online with the help of a reward estimator in phases.

3.2 Reliability and Learnability of Feedback

In interactive NLP, it is unrealistic to expect anything else than *bandit feedback* from a human user interacting with a chatbot, automatic summarization tool, or commercial machine translation system. That is, users of such systems will only provide a reward signal to the one output that is presented to them, and cannot be expected to rate a multitude of outputs for the same input. As a result, the feedback is very sparse in relation to the size of the output space.

Ideally, the user experience should not be disrupted through feedback collection. Non-intrusive interface options for example allow for corrections of the output ("post-edits" in the context of machine translation) as a negative signal, or recording whether the output is copied and/or shared without changes, which may be interpreted as a positive signal. However, the signal might be *noisy*, since the notion of output quality for natural language generation tasks is not a well-defined function to start with: Each input might have many possible valid outputs, each of which humans may judge differently, depending on many contextual and personal factors. In machine translation evaluation for instance, inter-rater agreements have traditionally been reported as low (Turian et al., 2003; Carl et al., 2011; Lommel et al., 2014), especially when quality estimates are collected from non-professional

raters (Callison-Burch, 2009). Similar observations have been made for other text generation tasks (Godwin and Piwek, 2016; Verberne et al., 2018). Nguyen et al. (2017) illustrated how badly machine translation systems can handle human-level noise in direct feedback for online RL with simulations. The level of noise in real-world human feedback may be so high that it prevents learning completely, as for example experienced in e-commerce machine translation logs (Kreutzer et al., 2018a). The issue is even higher in dialogue generation where there are a plenitude of acceptable responses (Pang et al., 2020). To this aim, inverse RL has been proposed to infer reward functions from responses indirectly (Takanobu et al., 2019).

Surprisingly, the question of how to best improve an RL agent in the scenario of learning from real-world human feedback has been scarcely researched. This might originate from many RL research environments coming with fixed reward functions. In the real world, however, there is rarely a clearly defined single reward function for which it would suffice optimizing for. The suggestions in Dulac-Arnold et al. (2019) seem straightforward: warm-starting agents to decrease sample complexity or using inverse reinforcement learning to recover reward functions from demonstrations (Wang et al., 2020) — but they require additional supervision signals that RL was supposed to alleviate.

When it comes to the question *which type of human feedback is most beneficial* for training an RL agent, one finds a lot of blanket statements, e.g., referring to the advantages of pairwise comparisons (Thurstone, 1927). For instance, learning from human pairwise preferences from humans has been advertised for summarization (Christiano et al., 2017; Stiennon et al., 2020) and language modeling (Ziegler et al., 2019), but the reliability of the signal has not been evaluated. An exception is the work of Kreutzer et al. (2018b) which is the first to investigate two crucial questions. The first question addresses which type of human feedback — pairwise judgments or cardinal feedback on a 5-point scale — can be given most *reliably* by human teachers. The second question investigates which type of feedback allows to learn reward estimators that best approximate human rewards and can be best integrated into an end-to-end RL-NLP task.

Regarding the first question, Kreutzer et al. (2018b) found that the common assumption — that pairwise comparisons are easier to judge than a single output on a Likert scale (Thurstone, 1927) — turned out to be false for the task of machine translation. Inter-rater reliability proved to be higher for 5-point ratings (Krippendorff's $\alpha = 0.51$) than for pairwise judgments ($\alpha = 0.39$). (Kreutzer et al., 2018b) explain two advantages that the Likert scale setup offers: (1) it is possible to standardize cardinal judgments for each rater to remove individual biases, (2) they offer an absolute anchoring for quality, while a preference rankings leave the overall positioning of the pair of outputs on a quality scale open. For pairwise judgments it is difficult or even impossible to reliably choose between two outputs that are similarly good or bad, e.g., differing by only a few words. Therefore, filtering out raters with low intra-rater reliability proved effective for absolute ratings, while filtering outputs with a high variance in ratings was most effective for pairwise ratings, yielding the final inter-rater reliability given above. Discarding rated outputs, however, reduces the size of the log to learn from, which is undesirable in settings where rewards are scarce or costly.

To answer the second question, Kreutzer et al. (2018b) found a neural machine translation system can be significantly improved using a reward estimator trained on only a few hundred cardinal user judgments. This work highlights that future research in real-world RL might have to involve studies in *user interfaces* or user experience, since the interfaces for feedback collection influence the reward function that RL agents learn from – and thereby the downstream task success. Collecting implicit feedback (Kreutzer et al., 2018a; Jaques et al., 2020) might offer a better user experience.

For the challenges discussed in Sections 3.1 and 3.2, a promising approach is to tackle the arguably simpler problem of learning a reward estimator from human feedback first, then provide unlimited learned feedback to generalize to unseen outputs in off-policy RL. However, risks of bias introduction and potential benefits for noise reduction through replacing user feedback by reward estimators are yet to be quantified.

4 Conclusion

There is large potential in NLP to leverage user interaction logs for system improvement. We discussed how algorithms for offline RL can offer promising solutions for this learning problem. However, specific challenges in offline RL arise due to the particular nature of NLP systems that collect human feedback in real-world applications. We presented cases where such challenges have been found and offered solutions that have helped. So far, the solutions have mainly been explored in the context of machine translation and semantic parsing. In the future, it will be interesting to explore further tasks and additional real-world use cases to find out how to best learn from human feedback.

References

Dzmitry Bahdanau, Philemon Brakel, Kelvin Xu, Anirudh Goyal, Ryan Lowe, Joelle Pineau, Aaron Courville, and Yoshua Bengio. 2017. An actor-critic algorithm for sequence prediction. In *5th International Conference on Learning Representations, ICLR*, Toulon, France.

H. Bastani, M. Bayati, and K. Khosravi. 2017. Exploiting the natural exploration in contextual bandits. *ArXiv e-prints*, 1704.09011.

Felix Berkenkamp, Matteo Turchetta, Angela Schoellig, and Andreas Krause. 2017. Safe model-based reinforcement learning with stability guarantees. In *Advances in Neural Information Processing Systems (NeurIPS)*, pages 908–918, Long Beach, California.

Léon Bottou, Jonas Peters, Joaquin Quiñonero-Candela, Denis X. Charles, D. Max Chickering, Elon Portugaly, Dipanakar Ray, Patrice Simard, and Ed Snelson. 2013. Counterfactual Reasoning and Learning Systems: The Example of Computational Advertising. *Journal of Machine Learning Research*, 14.

Chris Callison-Burch. 2009. Fast, cheap, and creative: Evaluating translation quality using Amazon's Mechanical Turk. In *Proceedings of the 2009 Conference on Empirical Methods in Natural Language Processing (EMNLP)*, Singapore.

Michael Carl, Barbara Dragsted, Jakob Elming, Daniel Hardt, and Arnt Lykke Jakobsen. 2011. The process of post-editing: a pilot study. *Copenhagen Studies in Language*, 41:131–142.

Olivier Chapelle and Lihong Li. 2011. An empirical evaluation of Thompson sampling. In *Advances in Neural Information Processing Systems (NeurIPS)*, Granada, Spain.

Leshem Choshen, Lior Fox, Zohar Aizenbud, and Omri Abend. 2020. On the weaknesses of reinforcement learning for neural machine translation. In *International Conference on Learning Representations (ICLR)*, Virtual.

Paul F. Christiano, Jan Leike, Tom Brown, Miljan Martic, Shane Legg, and Dario Amodei. 2017. Deep Reinforcement Learning from Human Preferences. In

Advances in Neural Information Processing Systems (NeurIPS), Long Beach, CA, USA.

Ernest Davis. 2016. AI amusements: the tragic tale of Tay the chatbot. *AI Matters*, 2(4):20–24.

Fabio De Bona, Stefan Riezler, Keith Hall, Massimiliano Ciaramita, Amaç Herdağdelen, and Maria Holmqvist. 2010. Learning dense models of query similarity from user click logs. In *Human Language Technologies: The 2010 Annual Conference of the North American Chapter of the Association for Computational Linguistics (HLT-ACL)*, Los Angeles, California.

Miroslav Dudik, John Langford, and Lihong Li. 2011. Doubly robust policy evaluation and learning. In *Proceedings of the 28th International Conference on Machine Learning (ICML)*, Bellevue, WA.

Gabriel Dulac-Arnold, Daniel J. Mankowitz, and Todd Hester. 2019. Challenges of real-world reinforcement learning. *CoRR*, abs/1904.12901.

Keith Godwin and Paul Piwek. 2016. Collecting reliable human judgements on machine-generated language: The case of the QG-STEC data. In *Proceedings of the 9th International Natural Language Generation conference (INLG)*, Edinburgh, UK.

Braden Hancock, Antoine Bordes, Pierre-Emmanuel Mazaré, and Jason Weston. 2019. Learning from dialogue after deployment: Feed yourself, chatbot!

Alexander Hans, Daniel Schneegaß, Anton Maximilian Schäfer, and Steffen Udluft. 2008. Safe exploration for reinforcement learning. In *ESANN*, pages 143–148.

Ji He, Jianshu Chen, Xiaodong He, Jianfeng Gao, Lihong Li, Li Deng, and Mari Ostendorf. 2016. Deep reinforcement learning with a natural language action space. In *Proceedings of the 54th Annual Meeting of the Association for Computational Linguistics (ACL)*, Berlin, Germany.

Natasha Jaques, Asma Ghandeharioun, Judy Hanwen Shen, Craig Ferguson, Agata Lapedriza, Noah Jones, Shixiang Gu, and Rosalind Picard. 2020. Way off-policy batch deep reinforcement learning of human preferences in dialog.

Nan Jiang and Lihong Li. 2016. Doubly robust off-policy value evaluation for reinforcement learning. In *Proceedings of the 33rd International Conference on Machine Learning (ICML)*, New York, NY.

Kirthevasan Kandasamy, Yoram Bachrach, Ryota Tomioka, Daniel Tarlow, and David Carter. 2017. Batch policy gradient methods for improving neural conversation models. In *5th International Conference on Learning Representations (ICLR)*.

Augustine Kong. 1992. A note on importance sampling using standardized weights. Technical Report 348, Department of Statistics, University of Chicago, Illinois.

Julia Kreutzer, Shahram Khadivi, Evgeny Matusov, and Stefan Riezler. 2018a. Can neural machine translation be improved with user feedback? In *Proceedings of the 2018 Conference of the North American Chapter of the Association for Computational Linguistics: Human Language Technologies, Volume 3 (ACL)*.

Julia Kreutzer, Joshua Uyheng, and Stefan Riezler. 2018b. Reliability and learnability of human bandit feedback for sequence-to-sequence reinforcement learning. In *Proceedings of the 56th Annual Meeting of the Association for Computational Linguistics (ACL)*.

Tsz Kin Lam, Julia Kreutzer, and Stefan Riezler. 2018. A reinforcement learning approach to interactive-predictive neural machine translation. In *Proceedings of the 21st Annual Conference of the European Association for Machine Translation (EAMT)*, Alicante, Spain.

John Langford, Alexander Strehl, and Jennifer Wortman. 2008. Exploration scavenging. In *Proceedings of the 25th International Conference on Machine Learning (ICML)*, Helsinki, Finland.

Carolin Lawrence, Pratik Gajane, and Stefan Riezler. 2017a. Counterfactual Learning for Machine Translation: Degeneracies and Solutions. In *Proceedings of the NIPS WhatIf Workshop*, Long Beach, California, USA.

Carolin Lawrence and Stefan Riezler. 2018. Improving a Neural Semantic Parser by Counterfactual Learning from Human Bandit Feedback. In *Proceedings of the 56th Annual Meeting of the Association for Computational Linguistics (ACL)*, Melbourne, Australia.

Carolin Lawrence, Artem Sokolov, and Stefan Riezler. 2017b. Counterfactual Learning from Bandit Feedback under Deterministic Logging : A Case Study in Statistical Machine Translation. In *Proceedings of the 2017 Conference on Empirical Methods in Natural Language Processing (EMNLP)*, Copenhagen, Denmark.

Jiwei Li, Will Monroe, Alan Ritter, Dan Jurafsky, Michel Galley, and Jianfeng Gao. 2016. Deep reinforcement learning for dialogue generation. In *Proceedings of the 2016 Conference on Empirical Methods in Natural Language Processing (EMNLP)*, Austin, Texas. Association for Computational Linguistics.

Arle Lommel, Maja Popovic, and Aljoscha Burchardt. 2014. Assessing inter-annotator agreement for translation error annotation. In *MTE: Workshop on Automatic and Manual Metrics for Operational Translation Evaluation*.

Khanh Nguyen, Hal Daumé III, and Jordan Boyd-Graber. 2017. Reinforcement learning for bandit neural machine translation with simulated human feedback. In *Proceedings of the 2017 Conference on Empirical Methods in Natural Language Processing (EMNLP)*.

Rodrigo Nogueira and Kyunghyun Cho. 2017. Task-oriented query reformulation with reinforcement learning. In *Proceedings of the 2017 Conference on Empirical Methods in Natural Language Processing (EMNLP)*, Copenhagen, Denmark.

Bo Pang, Erik Nijkamp, Wenjuan Han, Linqi Zhou, Yixian Liu, and Kewei Tu. 2020. Towards holistic and automatic evaluation of open-domain dialogue generation. In *Proceedings of the 58th Annual Meeting of the Association for Computational Linguistics (ACL)*, Online.

Doina Precup, Richard S. Sutton, and Satinder P. Singh. 2000. Eligibility traces for off-policy policy evaluation. In *Proceedings of the Seventeenth International Conference on Machine Learning (ICML)*, San Francisco, CA.

Pablo Rivas, Kerstin Holzmayer, Cristian Hernandez, and Charles Grippaldi. 2018. Excitement and concerns about machine learning-based chatbots and talkbots: A survey. In *2018 IEEE International Symposium on Technology and Society (ISTAS)*, pages 156–162. IEEE.

Paul R. Rosenbaum and Donald B. Rubin. 1983. The central role of the propensity score in observational studies for causal effects. *Biometrika*, 70(1).

Artem Sokolov, Julia Kreutzer, Stefan Riezler, and Christopher Lo. 2016. Stochastic structured prediction under bandit feedback. In *Advances in Neural Information Processing Systems (NeurIPS)*, Barcelona, Spain.

Nisan Stiennon, Long Ouyang, Jeff Wu, Daniel M. Ziegler, Ryan Lowe, Chelsea Voss, Alec Radford, Dario Amodei, and Paul Christiano. 2020. Learning to summarize from human feedback.

Alexander L. Strehl, John Langford, Lihong Li, and Sham M. Kakade. 2010. Learning from logged implicit exploration data. In *Advances in Neural Information Processing Sytems (NIPS)*, Vancouver, Canada.

Adith Swaminathan and Thorsten Joachims. 2015. The self-normalized estimator for counterfactual learning. In *Advances in Neural Information Processing Systems (NIPS)*, Montreal, Canada.

Ryuichi Takanobu, Hanlin Zhu, and Minlie Huang. 2019. Guided dialog policy learning: Reward estimation for multi-domain task-oriented dialog. In *Proceedings of the 2019 Conference on Empirical Methods in Natural Language Processing and the 9th International Joint Conference on Natural Language Processing (EMNLP-IJCNLP)*, Hong Kong, China.

Philip S. Thomas and Emma Brunskill. 2016. Data-efficient off-policy policy evaluation for reinforcement learning. In *Proceedings of the 33nd International Conference on Machine Learning (ICML)*, New York, NY.

Louis Leon Thurstone. 1927. A law of comparative judgement. *Psychological Review*, 34:278–286.

Gaurav Trivedi, Esmaeel R Dadashzadeh, Robert M Handzel, Wendy W Chapman, Shyam Visweswaran, and Harry Hochheiser. 2019. Interactive NLP in clinical care: Identifying incidental findings in radiology reports. *Applied clinical informatics*, 10(4):655.

Joseph P Turian, Luke Shea, and I Dan Melamed. 2003. Evaluation of machine translation and its evaluation. *Proceedings of MT Summit*, pages 386–393.

Suzan Verberne, Emiel Krahmer, Iris Hendrickx, Sander Wubben, and Antal van den Bosch. 2018. Creating a reference data set for the summarization of discussion forum threads. *Language Resources and Evaluation*, 52(2):461–483.

Jingkang Wang, Yang Liu, and Bo Li. 2020. Reinforcement learning with perturbed rewards. In *AAAI*, New York, New York.

Li Zhou, Kevin Small, O. Rokhlenko, and C. Elkan. 2017. End-to-end offline goal-oriented dialog policy learning via policy gradient. *ArXiv*, abs/1712.02838.

Daniel M. Ziegler, Nisan Stiennon, Jeffrey Wu, Tom B. Brown, Alec Radford, Dario Amodei, Paul Christiano, and Geoffrey Irving. 2019. Fine-tuning language models from human preferences. *arXiv preprint arXiv:1909.08593*.

Mode recovery in neural autoregressive sequence modeling

Ilia Kulikov
New York University
`kulikov@cs.nyu.edu`

Sean Welleck
University of Washington

Kyunghyun Cho
New York University
CIFAR Fellow in Learning
in Machines & Brains

Abstract

Despite its wide use, recent studies have revealed unexpected and undesirable properties of neural autoregressive sequence models trained with maximum likelihood, such as an unreasonably high affinity to short sequences after training and to infinitely long sequences at decoding time. We propose to study these phenomena by investigating how the modes, or local maxima, of a distribution are maintained throughout the full *learning chain* of the ground-truth, empirical, learned and decoding-induced distributions, via the newly proposed *mode recovery cost*. We design a tractable testbed where we build three types of ground-truth distributions: (1) an LSTM based structured distribution, (2) an unstructured distribution where probability of a sequence does not depend on its content, and (3) a product of these two which we call a semi-structured distribution. Our study reveals both expected and unexpected findings. First, starting with data collection, mode recovery cost strongly relies on the ground-truth distribution and is most costly with the semi-structured distribution. Second, after learning, mode recovery cost from the ground-truth distribution may increase or decrease compared to data collection, with the largest cost degradation occurring with the semi-structured ground-truth distribution. Finally, the ability of the decoding-induced distribution to recover modes from the learned distribution is highly impacted by the choices made earlier in the learning chain. We conclude that future research must consider the entire learning chain in order to fully understand the potentials and perils and to further improve neural autoregressive sequence models.

1 Introduction

Neural autoregressive sequence modeling has become the standard approach to modeling sequences in a variety of natural language processing applications (Aharoni et al., 2019; Brown et al., 2020; Roller et al., 2020). In this modeling paradigm, the probability of a sequence is decomposed into the product of the conditional probability of each token given the previous tokens. Each conditional probability is modeled by a shared neural network, typically implemented as a recurrent neural network (Hochreiter and Schmidhuber, 1997) or a transformer (Vaswani et al., 2017).

Despite its success, recent studies have identified peculiarities in neural autoregressive sequence models. Lee et al. (2018) identify *hallucinations* in neural machine translation, in which a well-trained model suddenly generates a nonsense translation when a rare token is artificially introduced to a source sentence. Stahlberg and Byrne (2019) observe that a vast portion of probability mass is concentrated on the *empty sequence* in neural machine translation, although the models they studied were never presented with empty sequences during training. Holtzman et al. (2019) report that large-scale language models often produce pathological sequences with many *n-gram repetitions*, at a rate which far exceeds that of the training data. Welleck et al. (2020a) show that neural language models can generate *infinite-length sequences* despite being trained on only finite sequences.

A common theme underlying these findings is that well-trained models can assign unreasonably high probabilities to sequences that are dissimilar to any sequence from the training set. In particular, the *modes* of the model's distribution appear to be undesired, implying that the model failed to *recover* the modes of the empirical distribution, which we term *mode recovery degradation*. The situation is further complicated by the fact that we only approximate the model's modes with a decoding algorithm, so it is unclear whether the decoding algorithm, the model, or even the data

Proceedings of the 5th Workshop on Structured Prediction for NLP, pages 44–52
August 1–6, 2021. ©2021 Association for Computational Linguistics

collection is at fault.

In this paper, we isolate and study mode recovery degradation by characterizing each stage of neural sequence modeling as inducing a new sequence distribution, then directly analyzing each distribution's modes. With this approach, we diagnose at what stage, and to what extent, sequences receive unreasonably high probabilities. To do so, we first define a *learning chain* that consists of the *ground-truth* distribution, the *empirical* distribution induced by data collection, the *learned* distribution, and the *decoding-induced* distribution. We then quantify the extent to which the most probable sequences under each distribution match the most probable sequences under the ground-truth distribution by defining a *mode recovery cost*, which measures how expensive it is for a later distribution to recover the most probable sequences of an earlier distribution in the chain.

In summary, we find that mode recovery cost is non-trivial at each part of the neural autoregressive learning pipeline. The pattern of how mode recovery changes heavily depends on the properties of the ground-truth distribution. In particular, when the ground-truth distribution is parameterized as a product of highly structured distribution based on LSTM neural network and unstructured distribution where the probability of every sequence is sampled independently from all the others, its modes are more costly to recover. Furthermore, the ability of a decoding algorithm to recover modes is also dependent upon all choices made earlier in the chain including the underlying ground-truth distribution, even in the case of modes of the learned distribution. These observations make a meaningful step towards better understanding of mode degradation in neural autoregressive sequence modeling.

2 Neural autoregressive sequence modeling

We consider the problem of modeling a distribution $p^*(\mathbf{s})$ over variable-length, discrete sequences $\mathbf{s}$. Formally, $\mathbf{s} \in \Sigma^l$, where $l \in \{1, 2, \ldots, L\}$, Σ is a finite set of tokens, and $\Omega \subset \bigcup_{l=1}^{L} \Sigma^l$ denotes the space of all possible sequences. Every sequence $\mathbf{s} \in \Omega$ ends with a special token $\langle \text{eos} \rangle \in \Sigma$ which only appears at the end of each sequence.

In neural autoregressive sequence modeling, we model the distribution $p^*(\mathbf{s})$ as $p_\theta(\mathbf{s}) = \prod_{t=1}^{|\mathbf{s}|} p_\theta(s_t|s_{<t})$, with each conditional distribution parameterized by a shared neural network.

Maximum likelihood. To learn the model, we use maximum likelihood estimation (MLE), which trains the model p_θ to maximize the log-likelihood of a set of training sequences $D = \{\mathbf{s}^1, \ldots, \mathbf{s}^N\}$:

$$\arg\max_\theta \frac{1}{N} \sum_{n=1}^{N} \sum_{t=1}^{L^n} \log p_\theta(s_t^n|s_{<t}^n). \quad (1)$$

Approximate decoding. Given a trained model, we obtain a set of highly probable sequences. In practice, this problem is often intractable due to the size of Ω, which grows exponentially in sequence length. As a result, we resort to approximating the optimization problem using a decoding algorithm that returns a set of k sequences $\mathcal{F}(p_\theta; \gamma)$, where $\mathcal{F}$ denotes the decoding algorithm, and γ denotes its hyper-parameters. Concretely, we consider two decoding approaches: a *deterministic* decoding algorithm that produces a set of sequences using beam search with beam-width k, and a *stochastic* decoding algorithm that forms a set of sequences using ancestral sampling until k unique sequences are obtained.[1] We refer readers to Welleck et al. (2020a) for detailed descriptions of those decoding algorithms.

Learning chain. The neural autoregressive sequence modeling approach consists of four probability distributions, which together form a *learning chain*. The first distribution is the *ground-truth distribution* $p^*(\mathbf{s})$. This distribution is almost always unknown and is assumed to be highly complicated. Second, the dataset used in maximum likelihood (Eq. 1) determines an *empirical distribution*,

$$p_{\text{emp}}(\mathbf{s}) = \frac{1}{|D|} \sum_{\mathbf{s}' \in D} \mathbb{I}(\mathbf{s} = \mathbf{s}'), \quad (2)$$

where D is a set of sequences drawn from the ground-truth distribution p^* and $\mathbb{I}$ is the indicator function. The third distribution is the *learned distribution* p_{model} captured by a neural autoregressive model trained on D.

Finally, we introduce the *decoding-induced distribution* $p_\mathcal{F}$, which allows us to compare the set of probable sequences obtained with a decoding algorithm $\mathcal{F}$ against highly probable sequences in the ground-truth, empirical, and learned distributions. Specifically, we turn this set into the distribution

$$p_\mathcal{F}(\mathbf{s}) = \begin{cases} \frac{1}{Z} p_\theta(\mathbf{s}) & \mathbf{s} \in \mathcal{F}(p_\theta; \gamma), \\ 0 & \mathbf{s} \notin \mathcal{F}(p_\theta; \gamma), \end{cases} \quad (3)$$

---

[1] Ancestral sampling recursively samples $s_t \sim p_\theta(s_t|s_{<t})$.

where $Z = \sum_{\mathbf{s}' \in \mathcal{F}(p_\theta; \gamma)} p_\theta(\mathbf{s}')$. Each sequence is weighted according to the model's probability, which reflects the practice of ordering and sampling beam search candidates by their probabilities.

There is a natural order of dependencies among these four distributions in the learning chain, $p^* \overset{\text{data collection}}{\succ} p_{\text{emp}} \overset{\text{learning}}{\succ} p_{\text{model}} \overset{\text{decoding}}{\succ} p_{\mathcal{F}}$. We are interested in how a distribution in the later part of the chain recovers the highly probable sequences of an earlier distribution. To study this, we next introduce the notion of *mode recovery*.

3   Mode recovery

Mode sets   We define a *k-mode set* as a set of top-k sequences under a given distribution:

$$\mathcal{S}_k(p) = \text{argtop-k}_{\mathbf{s} \in \Omega}\, p(\mathbf{s}).$$

argtop-k selects all the elements within Ω whose probabilities $p(\mathbf{s})$ are *greater than* the probability assigned to the $(k+1)$-st most likely sequence, which could result in fewer than k sequences. This is due to potentially having multiple sequences of the same probability.

Mode recovery cost.   We characterize the recovery of the modes of the distribution p by the distribution q as the cost required to recover the k-mode set $\mathcal{S}_k(p)$ using the distribution q. That is, how many likely sequences under q must be considered to recover all the sequences in the k-mode set of p.

Formally, given a pair of distributions p and q, we define the k-mode recovery cost from p to q as

$$\mathcal{O}_k(p\|q) = \min\left\{ k' \Big| \mathcal{S}_k(p) \subseteq \mathcal{S}_{k'}(q) \right\}. \quad (4)$$

The cost is minimized ($= |\mathcal{S}_k(p)|$) when the k-mode set of q perfectly overlaps with that of p. The cost increases toward $|\Omega|$ as the number of modes from q that must be considered to include the k-mode set from p increases. The cost is maximized ($=|\Omega|$) when the top-k set $\mathcal{S}_k(p)$ of p is not a subset of the support of the distribution q.

The limited support of q.   As mentioned earlier, the mode recovery cost $\mathcal{O}_k(p\|q)$ is ill-defined when the support of the distribution q, $\text{supp}(q)$, is not a super-set of the k-mode set of the distribution p . In this situation, we say that the distribution q fails to recover modes from the k-mode set of the distribution p. In particular, this happens with decoding-induced distributions because

of their limited support, which is equal to the size of the candidate set of sequences $\mathcal{F}(p_\theta, \gamma)$.

We introduce the k-mode set overlap $\mathcal{I}_k(p\|q) = |\mathcal{S}_k(p) \cap \text{supp}(q)|$, which equals the size of the intersection between the k-mode set of the distribution p and the support of the distribution q. The k-mode set overlap is maximized and equals $|\mathcal{S}_k(p)|$ when the mode recovery is successful. We call it a recovery failure whenever the overlap is smaller than $|\mathcal{S}_k(p)|$. We use k-mode set overlap only when mode recovery fails, because it is not able to detect if the modes from the corresponding k-mode set have high probability under the induced distribution.

4   Why do we study mode recovery?

The recent success of neural sequence modeling has operated on the assumption that we can find sequences that are reasonably similar to training sequences by fitting a neural autoregressive model to maximize the log-probabilities of the training sequences (maximum-likelihood learning) and searching for the most likely sequences under the trained model (maximum a posteriori inference). However, recent studies suggest that the most likely sequences may not resemble training sequences at all. For instance, the learning stage can yield a distribution p_{model} which places high probability on empty (Stahlberg and Byrne, 2019) or repetitive (Holtzman et al., 2019) sequences, while the decoding stage can yield a distribution $p_{\mathcal{F}}$ which places non-zero mass on infinite-length sequences (Welleck et al., 2020a).

As a result, various workarounds have been proposed in the form of alternative learning or decoding algorithms (Andor et al., 2016; Sountsov and Sarawagi, 2016; Murray and Chiang, 2018; Welleck et al., 2020b; Welleck and Cho, 2020; Martins et al., 2020; Deng et al., 2020; Basu et al., 2021; Shi et al., 2020). A particularly relevant work by Eikema and Aziz (2020) argues that the modes of neural sequence models are *inadequate* and thus we must discard maximum-a-posteriori inference altogether. Rather than advocating for a particular solution, we instead seek an understanding of *why* the conventional approach displays these peculiar behaviors. While we do not claim to provide a full explanation, the first step is developing a way of quantifying the problem, then localizing it. To this end, we develop the mode recovery cost and measure it along the learning chain

$p^* \succ p_{\mathrm{emp}} \succ p_{\mathrm{model}} \succ p_{\mathcal{F}}$. This focus on modes departs from the conventional focus on evaluating the full distribution with a probabilistic divergence.

Mode recovery vs. probabilistic divergence. Mode recovery is related to but distinct from a probabilistic divergence. Often a probabilistic divergence is designed to consider the full support of one of two distributions between which the divergence is computed. For each point within this support, a probabilistic divergence considers the ratio, or difference, between the actual probabilities/densities assigned by the two distributions. For instance, the KL divergence $\mathrm{KL}(p\|q)$ computes $\sum_{x \sim p} p(x) \log p(x)/q(x)$. Another example is the total variation (TV) distance, which is equivalent to $\sum_{\omega \in \Omega} |p(\omega) - q(\omega)|/2$ when the sample set Ω is finite. The TV distance considers the entire sample set and computes the cumulative absolute difference between the probabilities assigned to each event by two distributions.

We find mode recovery more interesting than probabilistic divergence in this paper, because our goal is to check whether a decision rule, that is to (approximately) choose the most likely sequence based on an available distribution, changes as we follow the chain of induced distributions. Furthermore, we are not interested in how precisely unlikely sequences are modeled and what probabilities they are being assigned. We thus fully focus on mode recovery in this paper.

5 A testbed for evaluating mode recovery

It is intractable to measure mode recovery cost (Eq. 4) on real-world datasets that are popular in neural sequence modeling, e.g. wikitext-103 (Merity et al., 2016) given the exponential growth of the sequence space with sequence length. For example, the training part of Wikitext-103 consists of 28k sequences with 3.5k tokens, each drawn from a vocabulary of 267k tokens. Furthermore, these datasets do not provide access to the ground-truth distribution, which prevents us from computing any recovery cost involving p^*.

In order to allow exact computations of mode recovery cost, we design a controllable testbed. This testbed consists of (1) the ground-truth distribution, which permits explicit control over the structuredness, (2) the data collection step, which controls the complexity of the empirical distribution, (3) the learning step, which allows us to induce the learned distribution with neural autoregressive models, and (4) the decoding step, where the decoding algorithm induces the approximation of the learned distribution. In the rest of this section we describe each distribution in detail.

We set the size of the sequence space of the testbed so that all computations are feasible. We limit the vocabulary size $|\Sigma|$ to 7 tokens and use a maximum sequence length L of 10 tokens. This results in a sequence space size $|\Omega|$ of around 12 million sequences.

Ground-truth distribution. We define each ground-truth distribution as a product of two components:

$$p_\alpha^*(\mathbf{s}) \propto p_\theta(\mathbf{s})^\alpha p(\mathbf{s}; \mu, \sigma)^{(1-\alpha)},$$

where $p_\theta(\mathbf{s})$ is an autoregressive distribution with parameters θ. The probability $p(\mathbf{s}; \mu, \sigma)$ is constructed by $p(\mathbf{s}; \mu, \sigma) \propto \exp(x(\mathbf{s}))$, where $x(\mathbf{s}) \sim$ Laplace(μ, σ) is a fixed random sample for each $\mathbf{s}$, and $\alpha \in [0, 1]$.

We implement p_θ using a randomly initialized LSTM neural network, with two layers and 512 LSTM units in every layer. We build $p(\mathbf{s}; \mu, \sigma)$ with $\mu = 0.0$ and $\sigma = 1.0$.

We build the ground-truth distribution to reflect some properties of real data. First, real data has strong statistical dependencies among the tokens within each sequence. We induce these dependencies by assuming that each sequence is produced from left to right by generating each token conditioned on the previously generated sub-sequences of tokens. We implement this procedure using the LSTM neural network.

Second, there exist exceptional sequences in real data which receive high probability even though those sequences do not reflect statistical dependencies mentioned above. We build another distribution component in order to introduce exceptions in a way that there are no statistical dependencies in the given sequence. We use independent samples from a Laplace distribution as unnormalized probabilities of every sequence from the sequence space Ω. We thus ensure that there are no statistical dependencies among the tokens under this unstructured distribution.

We thus construct the product of two distributions described above so that it exhibits structured and unstructured aspects of the generating process. The mixing coefficient α allows us to interpolate between the heavily structured to heavily unstruc-

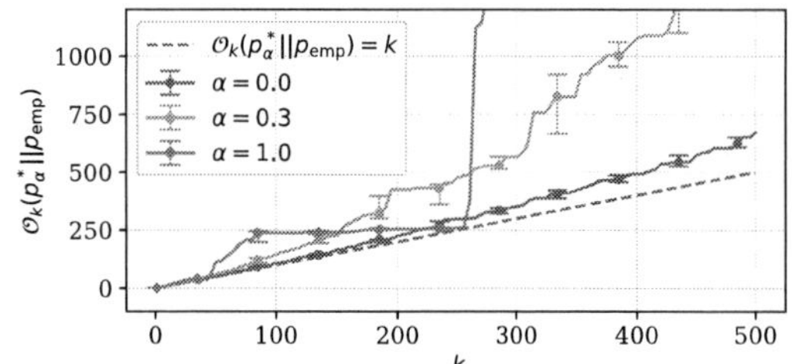

Figure 1: Mode recovery cost of the empirical distribution from the ground-truth distribution as a function of k while $N_{\text{train}} = 5 \times 10^5$.

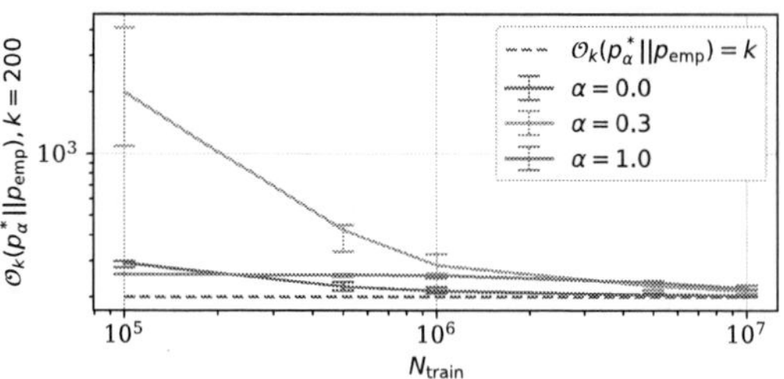

Figure 2: Mode recovery cost of the empirical distribution from the ground-truth distribution as a function of N_{train} while $k = 200$.

tured ground-truth distributions. We call it *semi-structured* when $0 < \alpha < 1$.

Empirical distribution. We create each empirical distribution p_{emp} (Eq. 2) by drawing samples with replacement from the ground-truth distribution. We sample a training multi-set and a validation multi-set, then form the empirical distribution with their union . We denote the size of the training dataset as N_{train}, and set the size of the validation set to $.05 \times N_{\text{train}}$.

Learned distribution. We obtain each learned distribution p_{model} by training an LSTM model on the training dataset D_{train} using maximum likelihood (Eq. 1). We vary the complexity of the learned distribution using the number of LSTM units of every layer of the LSTM neural network from the set $N_{\text{model hs}} \in \{128, 512\}$. Variable-length sequences are padded with a $\langle\text{pad}\rangle$ token in order to form equal-length batches of 5120 sequences. We use the Adam optimizer (Kingma and Ba, 2014) with a learning rate of 10^{-4}. We compute validation loss every 5×10^2 steps, and apply early stopping with a patience of 5 validation rounds based on increasing validation loss. We train the model for up to 2×10^4 steps. After training, the checkpoint with the lowest validation loss is selected to parameterize the learned distribution p_{model}.

Decoding-induced distribution. We form decoding-induced distributions (Eq. 3) using beam search and ancestral sampling. For beam search, we set $N_{\text{beam}} = 500$. For ancestral sampling, we sample sequences and discard duplicates until a given number of unique sequences, $N_{\text{anc}} = 500$, are obtained.

Randomness. To account for randomness that occurs when initializing the ground-truth distribution, sampling the empirical distribution, and using ancestral sampling during decoding, we run each configuration of the learning chain (i.e. ground-

truth, empirical, learned, and decoding-induced distributions) with 10 different random seeds, and report the median and 25-th and 75-th quantiles, if available, of each evaluation metric.

6 Mode recovery in the learning chain

We use our testbed to empirically study mode recovery degradation by measuring mode recovery cost in the data collection, learning, and decoding, stages of the learning chain. We use $k \leq 500$.

Data collection: recovering ground-truth modes with the empirical distribution. We start by asking: *does mode degradation happen during data collection?* We fix $N_{\text{train}} = 5 \times 10^5$ and compute mode recovery cost from the ground-truth distribution with the empirical distribution for the range of $k \leq 500$ presented in Fig.1 using three configurations of ground-truth distributions. It shows that mode recovery cost grows as k increases. Furthermore, we observe different patterns of mode recovery cost given each choice of the ground-truth distribution.

We observe distinct patterns of mode recovery with either structured ($\alpha = 1.0$) and unstructured ($\alpha = 0.0$) ground-truth distributions. We found that the structured ground-truth distribution assigns higher probabilities to shorter sequences because of LSTM neural network and autoregressive factorization. This implies that sequences which are sorted w.r.t. their probabilities are also sorted w.r.t. their lengths. Because of this property the empirical distribution can recover modes from the structured ground-truth distribution almost perfectly for particular k. In the case of the unstructured ground-truth distribution mode recovery cost is lower compared to other cases. This ground-truth distribution has no statistical dependencies within modes which makes it less interesting to us due to the lack of similarity with real data.

Finally, in the case of the semi-structured ground-

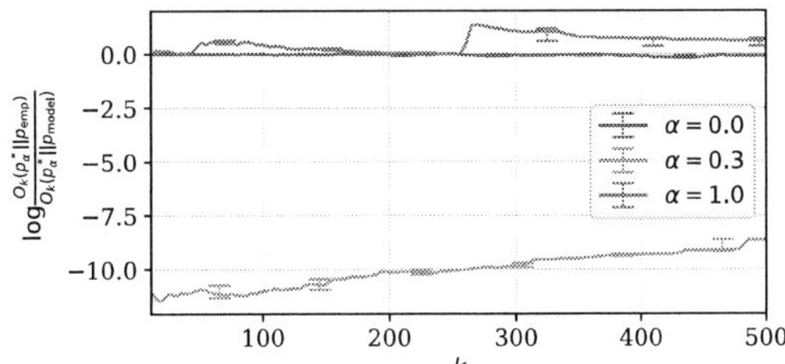

Figure 3: Mode recovery cost reduction log-rate between empirical and learned distributions from the ground-truth distribution as a function of k while $N_{\text{train}} = 5 \times 10^5$.

truth distribution ($\alpha = 0.3$) the cost of recovering its modes grows increasingly as k increases. In other words, empirical distributions recover modes from ground-truth distributions less effectively when latter exhibit statistical dependencies as well as many exceptional sequence probabilities.

Now we focus on the influence of the training set size N_{train} on mode recovery during data collection. We fix $k = 200$ and compute mode recovery cost from the ground-truth distribution using the empirical distribution when $N_{\text{train}} \in \{10^5, 5 \times 10^5, 10^6, 5 \times 10^6, 10^7\}$, shown in Fig.2. Mode recovery cost naturally decreases as we increase the number of training instances as seen on the right-most side of Fig.2. The left-most side is more interesting to us because it corresponds to values of N_{train} that reflect real world problems. For instance, in the case of $N_{\text{train}} = 10^5$ it is significantly more costly to recover modes from the semi-structured ground-truth distribution compared to both structured and unstructured variants. We thus conclude that mode recovery degradation happens already during data collection, and that parameterization of ground-truth distributions impacts mode recovery cost.

Learning: recovering modes with the learned distribution. The next stage in the chain is learning, $p_{\text{emp}} \succ_{\text{learning}} p_{\text{model}}$, in which we train a model using a training dataset with the expectation that the model will match the ground-truth distribution. Our experiments center on the question: *how does mode recovery degradation in the learning stage compare to that of the data collection stage?* For instance, we anticipate that the learned model will have a mode recovery cost that is at least as bad as that of the empirical distribution.

We measure the *mode recovery cost reduction log-rate* from empirical to learned distributions, $\log \frac{\mathcal{O}_k(p_\alpha^* \| p_{\text{emp}})}{\mathcal{O}_k(p_\alpha^* \| p_{\text{model}})}$. Fig.3 shows the reduction log-

rate as a function of k with fixed $N_{\text{train}} = 5 \times 10^5$, for three different ground-truth distributions. We observe three different cases, with a clear dependency on what kind of data was used during learning.

Learning with data coming from the unstructured ground-truth distribution ($\alpha = 0.0$) results in mode recovery cost reduction log-rate being close to zero. This implies that the underlying LSTM model is able to memorize the unstructured data points coming from the empirical distribution, but it can not recover any other modes from the ground-truth distribution.

With the structured ground-truth distribution ($\alpha = 1.0$), we observe positive log-rate for some values of k. This means that the learned distribution is able to recover modes of the ground-truth distribution at a lower cost than the empirical distribution does. Similarly to data collection stage, this largely happens due to the property of LSTM to put high probabilities on short sequences. The learned distribution's ability in mode recovery goes above that of the empirical distribution when there is a match between the parameterization of models behind the ground-truth distribution and the learned distribution.

In the case of the semi-structured ground-truth distribution ($\alpha = 0.3$), the learned distribution has severe mode recovery degradation even with smaller values of k (left-most side of Fig.3). The model is unable to perfectly learn an underlying dataset which has a few statistical exceptions within it.

In addition to our observations about recovering modes from ground-truth distributions, Fig.4 shows at what cost modes of each empirical distribution are recovered by the learned distribution as a function of N_{train}. The learned distribution recovers modes of the empirical distribution with the highest cost when the latter was induced using the semi-structured ground-truth distribution. Mode recovery cost of all empirical distributions naturally decreases as number of training instances N_{train} becomes unrealistically high. We conjecture that the combination of sequences with statistical dependencies and sequences which do not share any statistical dependencies in the dataset makes the learned distribution struggling at mode recovery from both ground-truth and empirical distributions.

We conclude that properties of ground-truth distributions have direct impacts on the ability of the

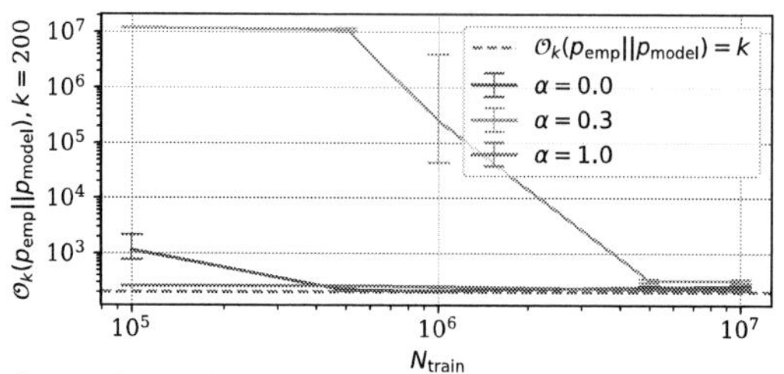

Figure 4: Mode recovery cost of the learned distribution from the empirical distribution as a function of N_{train} while $k = 200$.

learned distributions to recover modes from ground-truth and empirical distributions. Learning struggles to capture all patterns from the underlying distributions when the latter exhibit exceptions in statistical dependencies within data points.

Decoding: recovering modes with the decoding-induced distribution. The final stage in the learning chain is decoding, $p_{\text{model}} \succ_{\text{decoding}} p_{\mathcal{F}}$, in which we use a decoding algorithm $\mathcal{F}$ to obtain highly-probable sequences. We study both a *deterministic* decoding algorithm, implemented using beam search, and a *stochastic* decoding algorithm, implemented using ancestral sampling. Our experiments are centered on two questions: (1) *how do the choices made earlier in the learning chain affect the decoding behavior?* and (2) *how is this behavior affected by the choice of the decoding algorithm?*

We consider six different datasets that we train models on, each of which is a combination of the ground-truth distribution where $\alpha \in \{0.0, 0.3, 1.0\}$, and the number of training points $N_{\text{train}} \in \{5 \times 10^5, 5 \times 10^6\}$. Our previous analysis revealed each of those datasets leads to a substantially different ability of the learned distributions to recover modes from earlier distributions along the learning chain. We set $N_{\text{model hs}}$ to be equal to 512. Our choice of decoding algorithms results in decoding-induced distributions with a limited support. Hence the induced distribution $p_{\mathcal{F}}$ often fails to recover modes of distributions from the earlier stage of the chain especially as k increases. As we described in Sec. 3, we use the k-mode set overlap $\mathcal{I}_k(\cdot \| p_{\mathcal{F}})$ to examine the degree to which a given decoding algorithm $\mathcal{F}$ fails at mode recovery.

First, we study how well the decoding algorithm recovers modes from the learned distribution. Fig.5 shows k-mode set overlap between learned and decoding-induced distributions using both beam search (left) and ancestral sampling (right). Both algorithms fail increasingly more often as k increases.

Ancestral sampling fails substantially more often than beam search. This is expected given that ancestral sampling was not designed to find highly probable sequences, unlike beam search. Both of these decoding algorithms fail to recover modes from the learned distribution most when the learned distribution was obtained using the semi-structured ground-truth distribution ($\alpha = 0.3$), regardless of the size of the dataset. In other words, the choices made earlier along the learning chain impact the decoding-induced distribution's ability to recover modes from the learned distribution, regardless of which decoding algorithm was used.

Second, we investigate how the choice of the decoding algorithm influences the difference in how the decoding-induced distribution recovers modes of ground-truth and learned distributions. We thus look at the k-mode set overlap reduction from ground-truth to learned distributions ($\mathcal{I}_k(p_\alpha^* \| p_{\mathcal{F}}) - \mathcal{I}_k(p_{\text{model}} \| p_{\mathcal{F}})$) for both beam search and ancestral sampling. The positive overlap reduction in Fig.6 means that the decoding algorithm fails more to recover modes from the learned distribution than from the ground-truth distribution.

Each decoding algorithm shows a different pattern of the overlap reduction. Reduction is more or less flat and is close to zero for ancestral sampling regardless of the choice of the dataset. It is, however, different with beam search where we have three observations. First, the reduction overlap deviates from zero as k increases. Second, with the semi-structured ground-truth distribution ($\alpha = 0.3$) the overlap deviates most, which is then followed by the unstructured variant ($\alpha = 0.0$). Third, the number of training points N_{train} leads to significant difference in the case of the semi-structured distribution. Reduction overlap goes very negative with the smaller number of training instances, while the trend flips when we have ten times more data. We thereby conclude that the pattern of mode recovery degradation along the entire learning chain depends on the choice of the decoding algorithm.

7 Conclusion

In this paper, we studied the propensity of neural autoregressive sequence models to assign high probabilities to sequences that differ from those in the ground-truth distribution. To measure this phenomenon, we defined *mode recovery cost*, which measures a distribution's ability to recover the highly probable sequences of another distribution.

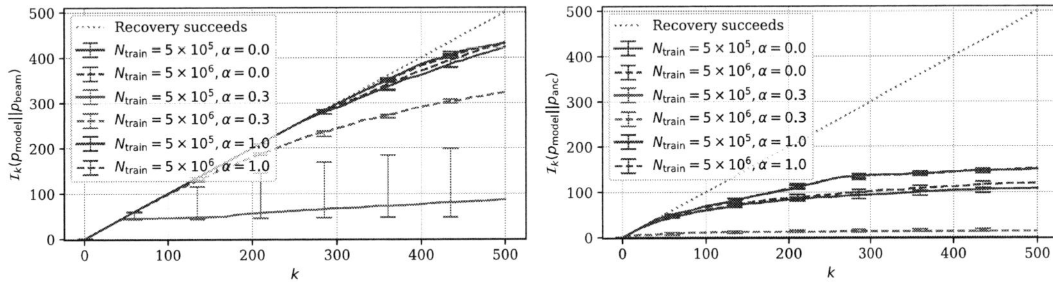

Figure 5: k-mode set overlap between the learned distribution and the decoding-induced distribution as a function of k. Choices made earlier in the learning chain (including ground-truth distribution, data collection and learning) affect the degree to which the decoding-induced distribution fails to recover modes from the learned distribution.

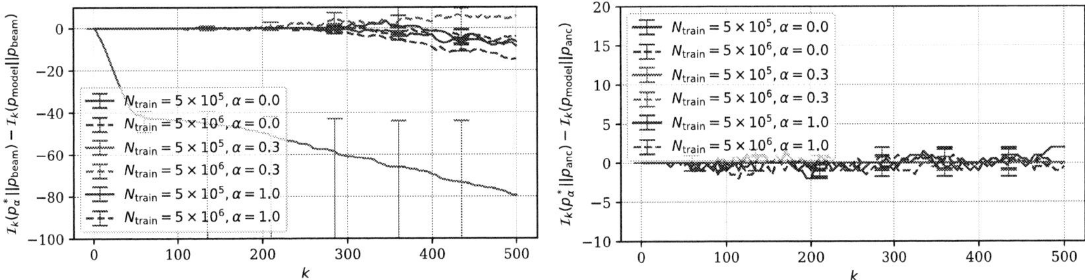

Figure 6: k-mode set overlap reduction from the ground-truth distribution to the learned distribution using the decoding-induced distribution as a function of k. The choice of the decoding algorithm affects the pattern of mode recovery degradation along the entire learning chain.

We developed a testbed for evaluating mode recovery cost throughout the entire learning chain.

We provided evidence of non-trivial mode recovery cost within this testbed, and observed that the increase in the cost relies heavily on the structuredness of the ground-truth distribution. Mode recovery from earlier distributions was more costly along the learning chain when the ground-truth distribution was constructed as a product of fully-structured and fully-unstructured distributions such that it reflects patterns in real data.

Mode recovery cost at each stage depended on all the choices made earlier at all the previous stages. The empirical distribution induced during data collection recovered modes from the ground-truth distribution imperfectly regardless of the dataset size. It was particularly high when we used the semi-structured ground-truth distribution. As expected, mode recovery cost was negatively correlated with a number of training instances.

Mode recovery after learning was directly affected by the choice of the ground-truth distribution as well. In general, the learned distribution failed to recover modes from the ground-truth distribution as well as the empirical distribution does. This trend flipped, however, when the learned distribution was parameterized identically to the ground-truth distribution. Distributions induced during decoding recovered modes of learned distributions with sig-

nificantly different costs depending on all choices made at previous stages of the learning chain. The choice of decoding algorithm was also found to influence patterns of mode recovery cost. Based on these observations, we conclude that we have to use the entire learning chain to study mode recovery in neural autoregressive sequence modeling.

Future directions. We highlight three main directions of research based on our findings and conclusions. First, mode recovery along the learning chain must be studied in the context of real world problems. To do so, there is a need for future work on approximation schemes of mode recovery cost computable in real tasks. Second, the relationship between the ground-truth and learned distributions may be changed to better match real-world cases, for instance by considering structured ground-truth distributions that are less similar to the learned model family, or unstructured components that are informed by sequence content. Third, we have considered standard practices of neural autoregressive modeling while constructing the learning chain. Extending the learning chain to study the effects of new approaches such as knowledge distillation (Kim and Rush, 2016) or back translation (Sennrich et al., 2016) is another fruitful direction for future research.

References

Roee Aharoni, Melvin Johnson, and Orhan Firat. 2019. Massively multilingual neural machine translation. *arXiv preprint arXiv:1903.00089*.

Daniel Andor, Chris Alberti, David Weiss, Aliaksei Severyn, Alessandro Presta, Kuzman Ganchev, Slav Petrov, and Michael Collins. 2016. Globally normalized transition-based neural networks. In *54th Annual Meeting of the Association for Computational Linguistics, ACL 2016 - Long Papers*.

Sourya Basu, Govardana Sachitanandam Ramachandran, Nitish Shirish Keskar, and Lav R. Varshney. 2021. Mirostat: A neural text decoding algorithm that directly controls perplexity. In *International Conference on Learning Representations*.

Tom B Brown, Benjamin Mann, Nick Ryder, Melanie Subbiah, Jared Kaplan, Prafulla Dhariwal, Arvind Neelakantan, Pranav Shyam, Girish Sastry, Amanda Askell, et al. 2020. Language models are few-shot learners. *arXiv preprint arXiv:2005.14165*.

Yuntian Deng, Anton Bakhtin, Myle Ott, Arthur Szlam, and Marc'Aurelio Ranzato. 2020. Residual energy-based models for text generation. In *International Conference on Learning Representations*.

Bryan Eikema and Wilker Aziz. 2020. Is MAP decoding all you need? the inadequacy of the mode in neural machine translation. In *Proceedings of the 28th International Conference on Computational Linguistics*, pages 4506–4520, Barcelona, Spain (Online). International Committee on Computational Linguistics.

S. Hochreiter and J. Schmidhuber. 1997. Long short-term memory. *Neural Computation*, 9:1735–1780.

Ari Holtzman, Jan Buys, Li Du, Maxwell Forbes, and Yejin Choi. 2019. The curious case of neural text degeneration. *arXiv preprint arXiv:1904.09751*.

Yoon Kim and Alexander M. Rush. 2016. Sequence-level knowledge distillation. *Proceedings of the 2016 Conference on Empirical Methods in Natural Language Processing*.

Diederik P Kingma and Jimmy Ba. 2014. Adam: A method for stochastic optimization. *arXiv preprint arXiv:1412.6980*.

Katherine Lee, Orhan Firat, Ashish Agarwal, Clara Fannjiang, and David Sussillo. 2018. Hallucinations in neural machine translation.

Pedro Henrique Martins, Zita Marinho, and André F. T. Martins. 2020. Sparse text generation. In *Proceedings of the 2020 Conference on Empirical Methods in Natural Language Processing (EMNLP)*, pages 4252–4273, Online. Association for Computational Linguistics.

Stephen Merity, Caiming Xiong, James Bradbury, and Richard Socher. 2016. Pointer sentinel mixture models.

Kenton Murray and David Chiang. 2018. Correcting length bias in neural machine translation. In *Proceedings of the Third Conference on Machine Translation: Research Papers*, pages 212–223, Brussels, Belgium. Association for Computational Linguistics.

Stephen Roller, Emily Dinan, Naman Goyal, Da Ju, Mary Williamson, Yinhan Liu, Jing Xu, Myle Ott, Kurt Shuster, Eric M Smith, et al. 2020. Recipes for building an open-domain chatbot. *arXiv preprint arXiv:2004.13637*.

Rico Sennrich, Barry Haddow, and Alexandra Birch. 2016. Improving neural machine translation models with monolingual data. *Proceedings of the 54th Annual Meeting of the Association for Computational Linguistics (Volume 1: Long Papers)*.

Xing Shi, Yijun Xiao, and Kevin Knight. 2020. Why neural machine translation prefers empty outputs.

Pavel Sountsov and Sunita Sarawagi. 2016. Length bias in encoder decoder models and a case for global conditioning. In *EMNLP 2016 - Conference on Empirical Methods in Natural Language Processing, Proceedings*.

Felix Stahlberg and Bill Byrne. 2019. On NMT search errors and model errors: Cat got your tongue? In *Proceedings of the 2019 Conference on Empirical Methods in Natural Language Processing and the 9th International Joint Conference on Natural Language Processing (EMNLP-IJCNLP)*, pages 3354–3360, Hong Kong, China. Association for Computational Linguistics.

Ashish Vaswani, Noam Shazeer, Niki Parmar, Jakob Uszkoreit, Llion Jones, Aidan N Gomez, Lukasz Kaiser, and Illia Polosukhin. 2017. Attention is all you need. *arXiv preprint arXiv:1706.03762*.

Sean Welleck and Kyunghyun Cho. 2020. Mle-guided parameter search for task loss minimization in neural sequence modeling.

Sean Welleck, Ilia Kulikov, Jaedeok Kim, Richard Yuanzhe Pang, and Kyunghyun Cho. 2020a. Consistency of a recurrent language model with respect to incomplete decoding. *arXiv preprint arXiv:2002.02492*.

Sean Welleck, Ilia Kulikov, Stephen Roller, Emily Dinan, Kyunghyun Cho, and Jason Weston. 2020b. Neural text generation with unlikelihood training. In *International Conference on Learning Representations*.

Using Hierarchical Class Structure to Improve Fine-Grained Claim Classification

Erenay Dayanik[1], André Blessing[1], Nico Blokker[2], Sebastian Haunss[2],
Jonas Kuhn[1], Gabriella Lapesa[1], and Sebastian Padó[1]

[1]IMS, University of Stuttgart, Germany
[2]SOCIUM, University of Bremen, Germany

Abstract

The analysis of public debates crucially requires the classification of political demands according to hierarchical *claim ontologies* (e.g. for immigration, a supercategory "Controlling Migration" might have subcategories "Asylum limit" or "Border installations"). A major challenge for automatic claim classification is the large number and low frequency of such subclasses. We address it by jointly predicting pairs of matching super- and subcategories. We operationalize this idea by (a) encoding soft constraints in the claim classifier and (b) imposing hard constraints via Integer Linear Programming. Our experiments with different claim classifiers on a German immigration newspaper corpus show consistent performance increases for joint prediction, in particular for infrequent categories and discuss the complementarity of the two approaches.

1 Introduction

Newspaper articles are an invaluable source for the analysis of public debates. In political science, it is common to manually annotate the articles by identifying *claims* (text spans which report a demand on a specific policy aspect), assigning them fine-grained *claim categories* from domain-specific *claim ontologies* and attributing them to *actors* (e.g., politicians or parties). Actors and claim categories together can be used to construct expressive *discourse networks* (Leifeld, 2016) for in-depth analysis of debate structure and dynamics.

In line with the trend of applying NLP methods to questions from political science (e.g., Bamman and Smith, 2015; Glavaš et al., 2019) claim classification has been framed as generic text classification (Padó et al., 2019). That study however addresses only coarse-grained categories and reports mixed results even at that level, with a macro F1 of 46. This is arguably due to the well-known problems of fine-grained classification: The larger the set of classes, the more data would be desirable, while in actuality, the number of instances per class shrinks (Mai et al., 2018; Chang et al., 2020).

Our paper aims at developing practically useful models of fine-grained claim classification. Its main proposal is to exploit the hierarchical nature of claim ontologies by jointly predicting (frequent) supercategories and (informative) subcategories. By enforcing consistency between the levels, the predictions can profit off each other. We experiment with two operationalizations of this idea. The first one, Hierarchical Label Encoding (HLE, Shimaoka et al. (2017a)) introduces "soft" constraints through parameter sharing between classes in the classifier. The second one, Integer Linear Programming (ILP, e.g., Punyakanok et al. (2004)) introduces "hard" constraints in a post-processing step.

Both methods can be applied to a range of claim classifier architectures. We present experiments with four architectures on a German manually annotated corpus from the so-called refugee crisis in Germany in 2015. We answer the following questions: Do HLE and ILP improve the performance in our experimental setup? (Yes.) Is there complementarity between them? (Yes.) Does the effect depend on the underlying architectures. (Broadly, no.) What types of classes is the improvement most pronounced for. (Low-frequency ones.)

2 Dataset and Claim Ontology

Our experiments are conducted on an extended version of the *DebateNet-migr15* (Lapesa et al., 2020).[1] This corpus comprises 1361 articles published in 2015 on the German quality newspaper *taz*. The corpus is annotated manually according to a two-level claim ontology developed by politi-

---

[1]For details on the availability of the dataset and code used in our experiments, see `mardy-spp.github.io`

53

Proceedings of the 5th Workshop on Structured Prediction for NLP, pages 53–60
August 1–6, 2021. ©2021 Association for Computational Linguistics

	Original corpus					Modified corpus			
Code	Label	f	n.sub	mean f.sub	Code	f	low	mid	high
1xx	Controlling Migration	998	16	62 ± 46.2	1xx	994	2	3	7
2xx	Residency	726	18	40 ± 41.2	2xx	726	4	4	4
3xx	Integration	475	15	31 ± 35.5	3xx	470	1	3	2
4xx	Domestic Security	230	9	25 ± 17.9	4xx	229	3	3	0
5xx	Foreign Policy	689	9	76 ± 17.8	5xx	686	3	2	3
6xx	Economy	194	12	16 ± 13.1	6xx	192	3	2	0
7xx	Society	749	19	39 ± 37.9	7xx	744	4	3	5
8xx	Procedures	676	20	33 ± 37.7	8xx	667	5	3	3
	(a)					(b)			

Table 1: (a): Claim distribution by supercategories: *Code*; *Label*; frequency (*f*); number of subcategories (*n.sub*); mean subcategory frequency with SD (*mean f.sub*). (b): Claim distribution for each supercategory after very infrequent classes are merged. low/mid/high represents the distribution of subcategory frequencies.

cal science experts for the migration domain. The corpus contains 3827 annotated textual spans, each of which is assigned one or more categories from the claim ontology described below: spans can be assigned multiple categories when the statements touch on more than one policy issue.

Claim ontology Policy debates are inherently complex, as a reflection of the complexity of the problems which the policy addresses: in our case, control of migration, but also integration of refugees, foreign policy, etc. In our case, the claim ontology consists of 100 subcategories which are grouped into 8 supercategories (cf. Table 1a). For example, 'border controls' and 'quota for refugees' are subcategories of the supercategory 'migration control'. The fine-grained annotation is crucial to build a satisfactory picture of a policy debate: what we are interested in is the position of certain politicians with respect to specific policy aspects over time (i.e., being in favor or against refugee quotas), while the supercategories are not expressive enough for the analysis of the debate itself. At the same time, Table 1a shows the drop in frequency between supercategories (in the hundreds) and subcategories (in the tens), with pronounced differences between categories, resulting in a clear modeling challenge. We return to this point in Section 5.

3 Basic Claim Classification

Given the properties described above, we model claim classification as multi-label classification. We follow previous work on coarse-grained claim classification (Padó et al., 2019) in comparing a set

of neural models, ranging from baselines to state-of-the-art architectures. All models are trained using cross entropy loss with the sigmoid activation function. All models except BERT use custom Fast-Text (Bojanowski et al., 2017) word embeddings pretrained on a German newswire corpus.[2]

LSTM This model passes the input through a single-layer LSTM. The final hidden state is used as input to a fully connected layer.

BiLSTM A single-layer Bidirectional LSTM (Graves et al., 2013) traverses the input. The final hidden states in both directions are concatenated and fed to a fully connected layer.

BiLSTM+Attention This model combines the BiLSTM architecture with the attention mechanism described in Shimaoka et al. (2017a). The input is fed to a single-layer BiLSTM. Then, the attention-weighted sum of the hidden states corresponding to the input sequence is fed to a fully connected layer.

BERT This is a pretrained BERT (Devlin et al., 2019) model trained solely on German corpora[3] and a fully connected layer which is trained while the BERT encoder is fine-tuned. After each input is encoded, we use the final hidden state of the first token, corresponding to the special token [CLS], as the contextualized representation of the input which serves as input to a fully connected layer.

---

[2]Further details regarding the architecture and training parameters can be found in the appendix.
[3]https://deepset.ai/german-bert

4 Integrating Hierarchical Class Structure

The obvious shortcoming of the model architectures sketched above is that they make the standard assumption of class independence – even though we know that the classes in claim classification are related. We therefore build on the idea that we can label all documents with both sub- and supercategories during training time, and then encourage the model to jointly predict categories at both levels *so that these predictions are consistent with one another*. The expectation is that this creates an incentive to learn better representations for the fine-grained classes. We now sketch two generally applicable methods that implement this idea.

Hierarchical Label Encoding (HLE). The idea behind this approach is to inject the inference relation between sub- and supercategories into the representation learning process. Following Shimaoka et al. (2017a), we create a binary square matrix, $S \in \{0,1\}^{l \times l}$, where l is the number of claim classes in dataset. Each cell in the matrix is filled with 1 either if the column class is subclass of or same as the row class, and filled with 0 otherwise. The matrix S is not updated during training and integrated into models by multiplying it by the weight matrix W of the final fully connected layer of each model: $p(y = 1) = \mathrm{sigm}(h(W^\top S)^\top)$ where $W \in \mathbb{R}^{l \times hs}$, $h \in \mathbb{R}^{1 \times hs}$, $|y| = l$, and hs is the size of the hidden state of (Bi)LSTM or BERT. HLE introduces parameter sharing between classes in the same hierarchy (e.g. 100 and 101), but does not guarantee that the prediction output contains both a super- and a subcategory.

Integer Linear Programming (ILP). ILP has been applied to enforce linguistically motivated constraints on predicted structures such as semantic roles (Punyakanok et al., 2004), dependency parsing (Riedel and Clarke, 2006), or entailment graphs (Berant et al., 2011). Formally, an integer linear program is an optimization problem over a set of integer variables $\mathbf{x}$, given a linear objective function with a set of coefficients $\mathbf{c}$ and a set of linear inequality (and equality) constraints (Schrijver, 1984):

$$\max \mathbf{c}^\top \mathbf{x} \qquad \text{so that } Ax \geq b$$

We use ILP to select the most likely legal output from the probabilities estimated by the classifiers.

Legal outputs are those where (a) for each predicted subcategory, the matching supercategory is predicted, and (b) for each predicted supercategory, at least one matching subcategory is predicted. We introduce a binary variable x_i for each supercategory and subcategory in the claim ontology, indicating whether this class is being predicted. This makes our task a binary optimization problem, a subclass of ILP. The coefficients c are given by the probability estimates of the neural claim classifiers (NCCs):

$$c_i = P_{\mathrm{NCC}}(x_i = 1)$$

The objective function is the log likelihood of the complete model output, including both predicted and non-predicted classes:

$$\sum_i \log c_i x_i + \log[1 - c_i](1 - x_i)$$

The first constraints we impose on the solution is that each predicted subcategory must be accompanied by the matching supercategory. Let sup(i) denote the supercategory for the subcategory i. Then this constraint can be formalized as:

$$\text{for each subcategory } x_i : x_i - x_{sup(i)} \leq 0$$

The second constraint is that each predicted supercategory is accompanied by at least one if its subcategories. Let subs(i) denote the set of subcategories for supercategory i. The constraint is:

$$\text{for each supercategory } x_i : x_i - \sum_{j \in subs(i)} x_j \leq 0$$

ILP has a complementary profile to HLE in enforcing hard constraints on the output, without propagating the errors back to representation learning.

5 Experimental Evaluation

Setup. We remove very infrequent subcategories in the dataset by applying a threshold of 20 instances. Smaller categories are merged with the preexisting subcategory x99, which exists for each supercategory as a 'catch-all' category for outlier cases. After filtering, there are 8 super- and 72 subcategories left in the dataset (cf. Table 1b). We experiment with four model variations: **Plain** (base claim classifiers as in Section 3); **ILP** and **HLE** as described in Section 4; and **ILP+HLE**.

We split our dataset to train (90%) test (10%) splits and run the experiments on our own cluster with two Nvidia GeForce 1080GTX Ti GPUs. For each experiment, we perform grid search guided by cross-validation on the training set to find the best hyperparameters. We report Precision, Recall and F1 scores weighted over all subcategories.

Main Results. Table 2 summarizes the results of our experiments. In the 'plain' setting, LSTM and BiLSTM perform significantly worse than BiL-STM+Attention and BERT. This finding is consistent with the generally observed benefit of attention and previous results by Padó et al. (2019).

The addition of ILP (2nd column) leads to inconsistent changes in precision but always yields better Recall and F-Scores. LSTM and BiLSTM still perform significantly worse than the other two models. When we switch to HLE, all metrics for all models are boosted significantly, showing that parameter sharing via the super/sub-category co-occurrence matrix is a successful across the board. We observe the largest improvement for BERT, where HLE yields an improvement of 12 points in F1, and leads to the overall highest Precision (0.75).

The last column (HLE + ILP) shows a substantial complementarity of the two methods: models consistently improve over both the HLE only and ILP only setting. Specifically, HLE+ILP models achieves better Recall scores than HLE models (+7 points on average) and better Precision (+8 points on average) scores than ILP models. The effect is least pronounced for the best architecture (BERT); nevertheless, BERT with HLE and ILP achieves the overall highest Recall (0.59) and F-Score (0.60), corresponding to an improvement of 13 points F1 compared to the 'plain' version. The fact that the F1 boost is fueled mainly by Recall is particularly promising because optimizing for Recall is the best strategy when NLP tools are employed in semi-automatic annotation (Ganchev et al., 2007; Ambati et al., 2011).

Frequency Band Analysis. As discussed in the introductory section, fine-grained classification struggles in particular with infrequent classes. We therefore ask how hierarchical class structure affects performance in relation to frequency. To do so, we analyze the performance of the best architecture (BERT), splitting the fine-grained categories into three equal-sized frequency bands.[4]

---

[4]Thresholds: high-frequency ($265 \geq f \geq 67$), mid-frequency ($65 \geq f \geq 40$) and low-frequency ($20 \geq f \geq 39$). Complete lists of the categories in the frequency bands and detailed results of other models are available in Table 5 and Table 6 in the appendix.

The results in Table 3 show that the prediction quality of plain BERT differs significantly across frequency bands. It fails badly in the low freq band (F1=0.1) while doing a fair job in the mid and high bands (F1=0.42 and 0.57, respectively). Again, we see consistent improvements for both ILP and HLE, but the improvements are more substantial for HLE, in particular for the low-freq band (+27 point F1). Combining HLE and ILP further increases Recall, but reduces Precision somewhat.[5]

In sum, we observe that both ILP and HLE improve fine-grained classification. The parameter sharing introduced by HLE particularly helps the lowest-frequency categories and increases both Precision and Recall. ILP generally boosts Recall by enforcing that both super- and a subcategories need to be predicted. There appears to be a mid-frequency "sweet spot" where this is particularly effective: Less frequent, and the probability estimates are not reliable enough; more frequent, the Precision–Recall trade-off is not worth it.

Qualitative Considerations. Finally, we investigate which subcategories benefit most from HLE and ILP in our best model (BERT). Table 4 again shows complementarity between HLE and ILP, indicating that a better combination of the two methods could lead to further improvements. HLE+ILP overlaps largely with HLE, mirroring the larger impact of HLE. Analysis of these classes shows that they belong to the mid and low frequency bands.

However, not all low and mid frequency classes profit equally. To explain this, we note that the fine-grained classes in the migration ontology differ substantially with regard to *concreteness*: While the high-level category 'Foreign policy' (5xx) contains relatively concrete sub-categories ('Enforcing Dublin III regulations' or 'Expanding the list of safe countries of origin'), the supercategory 'Society' (7xx) mostly consists of less manifest policy measures ('Uphold Human Rights', 'Oppose Xenophobia'). With regard to that distinction, the highest-gain subcategories are of the concrete kind (cf. Table 1): 106 ('Border defence'), 303 ('Forced integration'), 801 ('Constitutional law'), 807 ('Reducing bureaucracy'), 405 ('Counterterrorism'). Conversely, we do not find any subcategories of the less concrete supercategory 700 ('Society').

---

[5]We confirmed the relationship between frequency and performance with a correlation analysis to rule out a binning artifact. See Table 7 in the appendix.

Model	plain			ILP			HLE			HLE + ILP		
	P	R	F1	P	R	F1	P	R	F1	P	R	F1
LSTM	0.50	0.24	0.30	0.45	0.28	0.32	0.60	0.33	0.39	0.52	0.38	0.41
BiLSTM	0.51	0.26	0.32	0.51	0.33	0.38	0.57	0.30	0.36	0.63	0.42	0.48
BiLSTM+Att	0.67	0.39	0.46	0.63	0.42	0.48	0.69	0.41	0.48	0.66	0.46	0.51
BERT	0.61	0.42	0.47	0.56	0.50	0.50	**0.75**	0.52	0.59	0.66	**0.59**	**0.60**

Table 2: Test results (weighted averages for fine-grained claim classification) for four architectures and two methods to integrate class structure (integer linear programming, hierarchical label encoding). Best results bolded.

Freq band	plain			ILP			HLE			HLE + ILP		
	P	R	F1	P	R	F1	P	R	F1	P	R	F1
Low freq	0.10	0.10	0.10	0.18	0.14	0.15	0.58	0.31	**0.37**	0.48	0.31	0.35
Mid freq	0.58	0.36	0.42	0.65	0.47	0.50	0.77	0.55	0.62	0.71	0.63	**0.65**
High freq	0.73	0.51	0.57	0.60	0.58	0.58	0.78	0.56	0.62	0.67	0.63	**0.64**

Table 3: Detailed results for BERT architecture: break down by frequency bands of fine-grained classes (highest F1 score for each frequency band bolded).

Setting	Highest Improvement
ILP	204, 499, 507, 508, 803
HLE	106, 303, 314, 801, 807
ILP+HLE	106, 303, 405, 801, 807

Table 4: Subcategories that gain most in F1 score

6 Conclusion

This paper has identified automatic fine-grained claim classification as a crucial, but underaddressed, component of political discourse analysis. We have demonstrated that hierarchical class structure can be exploited to lift fine-grained claim classification to a usable level, showing robust improvements even for transformer architectures and in particular for low-frequency claim categories.

Addressing the low-frequency issue is particularly relevant in the broader context of the goals of political science. Political discourse unfolds over time, and every prominent issue starts out as infrequent. The true dynamics of debates can only be captured if the classifiers are able to pick up the less salient categories (Koopmans and Statham, 1999; Kossinets, 2006). Future work involves investigating these concerns on a wider range of datasets, as well as evaluating fine-grained claim classification for semi-automatic discourse network construction.

Acknowledgments

We acknowledge funding by Deutsche Forschungsgemeinschaft (DFG) through MARDY (Modeling Argumentation Dynamics) within SPP RATIO and by Bundesministerium für Bildung und Forschung (BMBF) through E-DELIB (Powering up e-deliberation: towards AI-supported moderation).

References

Bharat Ram Ambati, Rahul Agarwal, Mridul Gupta, Samar Husain, and Dipti Misra Sharma. 2011. Error detection for treebank validation. In *Proceedings of the 9th Workshop on Asian Language Resources*, pages 23–30, Chiang Mai, Thailand. Asian Federation of Natural Language Processing.

David Bamman and Noah A. Smith. 2015. Open extraction of fine-grained political statements. In *Proceedings of the 2015 Conference on Empirical Methods in Natural Language Processing*, pages 76–85, Lisbon, Portugal. Association for Computational Linguistics.

Jonathan Berant, Ido Dagan, and Jacob Goldberger. 2011. Global learning of typed entailment rules. In *Proceedings of the 49th Annual Meeting of the Association for Computational Linguistics: Human Language Technologies*, pages 610–619, Portland, Oregon, USA. Association for Computational Linguistics.

Piotr Bojanowski, Edouard Grave, Armand Joulin, and Tomas Mikolov. 2017. Enriching word vectors with subword information. *Transactions of the Association for Computational Linguistics*, 5:135–146.

Wei-Cheng Chang, Hsiang-Fu Yu, Kai Zhong, Yiming Yang, and Inderjit S. Dhillon. 2020. Taming pretrained transformers for extreme multi-label text classification. In *Proceedings of the 26th ACM SIGKDD International Conference on Knowledge Discovery; Data Mining*, KDD '20, page 3163–3171, New York, NY, USA. Association for Computing Machinery.

Jacob Devlin, Ming-Wei Chang, Kenton Lee, and Kristina Toutanova. 2019. BERT: Pre-training of deep bidirectional transformers for language understanding. In *Proceedings of the 2019 Conference of the North American Chapter of the Association for Computational Linguistics: Human Language Technologies, Volume 1 (Long and Short Papers)*, pages 4171–4186, Minneapolis, Minnesota. Association for Computational Linguistics.

Kuzman Ganchev, Fernando Pereira, Mark Mandel, Steven Carroll, and Peter White. 2007. Semi-automated named entity annotation. In *Proceedings of the Linguistic Annotation Workshop*, pages 53–56, Prague, Czech Republic. Association for Computational Linguistics.

Goran Glavaš, Federico Nanni, and Simone Paolo Ponzetto. 2019. Computational analysis of political texts: Bridging research efforts across communities. In *Proceedings of the 57th Annual Meeting of the Association for Computational Linguistics: Tutorial Abstracts*, pages 18–23, Florence, Italy. Association for Computational Linguistics.

Alex Graves, Navdeep Jaitly, and Abdel-rahman Mohamed. 2013. Hybrid speech recognition with deep bidirectional LSTM. In *2013 IEEE workshop on automatic speech recognition and understanding*, pages 273–278. IEEE.

Ruud Koopmans and Paul Statham. 1999. Political Claims Analysis: Integrating Protest Event and Political Discourse Approaches. *Mobilization: An International Quarterly*, 4(2):203–221.

Gueorgi Kossinets. 2006. Effects of missing data in social networks. *Social Networks*, 28(3):247–268.

Gabriella Lapesa, Andre Blessing, Nico Blokker, Erenay Dayanik, Sebastian Haunss, Jonas Kuhn, and Sebastian Padó. 2020. DEbateNet-mig15: Tracing the 2015 immigration debate in Germany over time. In *Proceedings of LREC*, pages 919–927, Online.

Philip Leifeld. 2016. *Policy Debates as Dynamic Networks: German Pension Politics and Privatization Discourse*. Campus Verlag, Frankfurt/New York.

Khai Mai, Thai-Hoang Pham, Minh Trung Nguyen, Tuan Duc Nguyen, Danushka Bollegala, Ryohei Sasano, and Satoshi Sekine. 2018. An empirical study on fine-grained named entity recognition. In *Proceedings of the 27th International Conference on Computational Linguistics*, pages 711–722, Santa Fe, New Mexico, USA. Association for Computational Linguistics.

Sebastian Padó, Andre Blessing, Nico Blokker, Erenay Dayanik, Sebastian Haunss, and Jonas Kuhn. 2019. Who sides with whom? towards computational construction of discourse networks for political debates. In *Proceedings of the 57th Annual Meeting of the Association for Computational Linguistics*, pages 2841–2847, Florence, Italy. Association for Computational Linguistics.

Vasin Punyakanok, Dan Roth, Wen-tau Yih, and Dav Zimak. 2004. Semantic role labeling via integer linear programming inference. In *COLING 2004: Proceedings of the 20th International Conference on Computational Linguistics*, pages 1346–1352, Geneva, Switzerland. COLING.

Sebastian Riedel and James Clarke. 2006. Incremental integer linear programming for non-projective dependency parsing. In *Proceedings of the 2006 Conference on Empirical Methods in Natural Language Processing*, pages 129–137, Sydney, Australia. Association for Computational Linguistics.

Alexander Schrijver. 1984. *Linear and Integer Programming*. John Wiley & Sons, New York.

Sonse Shimaoka, Pontus Stenetorp, Kentaro Inui, and Sebastian Riedel. 2017a. Neural architectures for fine-grained entity type classification. In *Proceedings of the 15th Conference of the European Chapter of the Association for Computational Linguistics: Volume 1, Long Papers*, pages 1271–1280, Valencia, Spain. Association for Computational Linguistics.

Sonse Shimaoka, Pontus Stenetorp, Kentaro Inui, and Sebastian Riedel. 2017b. Neural architectures for fine-grained entity type classification. In *Proceedings of the 15th Conference of the European Chapter of the Association for Computational Linguistics: Volume 1, Long Papers*, pages 1271–1280, Valencia, Spain. Association for Computational Linguistics.

Appendix

A   Results Details: Results by Frequency Bands for all Architectures

Table 5 presents Precision, Recall and F1 scores of models broken down for low, mid and high frequency bands. We observe similar patterns with other three models: (1) Prediction quality of models in plain setting differ significantly across frequency bands and all three models perform significantly worse on low frequency band and (2) Extending models with HLE and ILP leads to significantly better F1 scores on all frequency bands.

B   Results Details: Correlation Analyses

We calculate Spearman's correlation coefficient in order to investigate the relationship between amount of available data for each subcategory and

Model	Freq band	plain			ILP			HLE			HLE + ILP		
		P	R	F1	P	R	F1	P	R	F1	P	R	F1
LSTM	Low freq	0.19	0.07	0.10	0.23	0.08	0.12	0.32	0.11	0.16	0.33	0.18	0.21
	Mid freq	0.57	0.20	0.28	0.53	0.25	0.31	0.66	0.33	0.42	0.58	0.38	0.43
	High freq	0.53	0.29	0.35	0.47	0.34	0.37	0.64	0.37	0.42	0.54	0.42	0.45
BiLSTM	Low freq	0.24	0.10	0.13	0.35	0.16	0.20	0.15	0.05	0.07	0.27	0.13	0.16
	Mid freq	0.54	0.20	0.28	0.56	0.27	0.35	0.68	0.22	0.32	0.54	0.30	0.37
	High freq	0.56	0.32	0.37	0.52	0.39	0.43	0.61	0.38	0.44	0.57	0.44	0.47
BiLSTM Att	Low freq	0.10	0.07	0.07	0.23	0.13	0.14	0.17	0.10	0.10	0.24	0.11	0.13
	Mid freq	0.82	0.47	0.56	0.69	0.45	0.53	0.71	0.46	0.53	0.64	0.52	0.55
	High freq	0.74	0.42	0.50	0.69	0.47	0.53	0.79	0.45	0.54	0.75	0.51	0.57
BERT	Low freq	0.10	0.10	0.10	0.18	0.14	0.15	0.58	0.31	0.37	0.48	0.31	0.35
	Mid freq	0.58	0.36	0.42	0.65	0.47	0.50	0.77	0.55	0.62	0.71	0.63	0.65
	High freq	0.73	0.51	0.57	0.60	0.58	0.58	0.78	0.56	0.62	0.67	0.63	0.64

Table 5: Detail results for all architectures by frequency band

performance change of BERT model across settings further. For that, we measure the difference between BERT model's subcategory performances in plan and other settings as well as amount of data available for each subcategory. Table 6 shows which subcategory belongs to which frequency band and Table 7 shows Spearman's correlation coefficients. We observe high negative values almost always indicating that there is a strong negative correlation between the amount of data exist for a subcategory and amount of change in performance which means that infrequent classes gain most from ILP and HLE.

Frequency Band	Label					
LOW	111	199	201	209	213	214
	406	408	499	502	505	508
	602	603	605	701	706	707
	708	801	802	807	811	814
MID	106	107	109	204	211	212
	215	301	302	303	307	401
	402	405	503	509	601	699
	702	711	715	803	804	808
HIGH	101	102	104	105	108	110
	190	202	203	207	299	309
	399	501	504	507	703	705
	709	712	799	805	812	899

Table 6: Lists of the categories in the frequency bands

	PAIR	P	R	F
BERT	Plain - ILP	-0.20	-0.10	-0.20
	Plain - HLE	-0.24	-0.31	-0.29
	Plain - (ILP+HLE)	-0.28	-0.29	-0.32

Table 7: Spearman's correlation coefficient results between change in evaluation metrics and subcategory size for BERT model.

C Training Details

In the LSTM model, we set the number of hidden units to 500. We train 300-dimensional Fast-Text word embeddings on a corpus consisting of German Newspapers and use them as the input to LSTM. We use Adam with learning rate of 0.003 as optimizer. Batch size and number of epochs are set to 16 and 25 respectively.

In the BiLSTM model, we the set number of units to 500 in each direction and batch size to 16. The same 300-dimensional word embeddings as in the LSTM are used. The model is trained with Adam optimizer and a learning rate of 0.003 for 25 epochs.

In the BiLSTM+Attn model, we used the attention mechanism variant described in Shimaoka et al. (2017b). We set number of units to 500 in each direction and batch size to 16. We use the same 300-dimensional word embeddings used in LSTM and BiLSTM models, and train model for 20 epochs using Adam optimizer with learning rate of 0.003.

For the BERT model, we use a cased BERT variant[6] that was trained specifically for German with default parameters for the number of attention heads, hidden layers, and the number of hidden units are 12, 12, and 768, respectively. During fine-tuning, we use the Adam optimizer with learning rates of 5e-5, $\beta_1 = 0.9$, $\beta_2 = 0.999$, and set the maximum sequence length to 200, batch size to 16 and norm of maximum gradient to 1.0 and trained for 20 epochs.

Table 8 and Table 9 show the number of parameters in each model and average time required to

---

[6]https://deepset.ai/german-bert

	Parameter Numbers	
	Plain	HLE
LSTM	4,731,080	4,731,500
BiLSTM	6,375,080	6,376,000
BiLSTM Att	6,475,180	6,476,100
BERT	109,142,864	109,143,552

Table 8: Number of parameters in each model.

	Runtime (in Minutes)
LSTM	1.5
BiLSTM	2.2
BiLSTM Att	4.5
BERT	32.0

Table 9: Average runtime required to train each model

train each model used in our experiments respectively.

Hyperparameter search details We perform grid search for hyperparameter optimization and use the hyperparameters leading highest average F1 score during 5-Fold cross validation. Following lower and upper bounds have been applied during search for each hyperparameter: learning Rate [1e-4, 5e-2], epoch:[5, 25], batch size:[16, 32].

D   Details about Dataset

Figure 1 depicts the number of instances for each category.

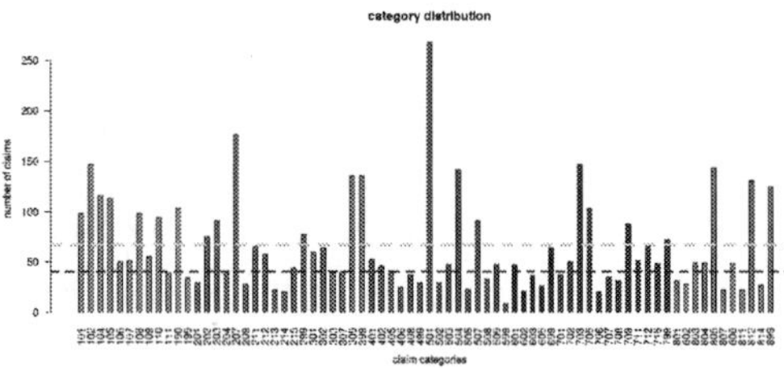

Figure 1: Claim distribution of subcategories. Green dotted line: boundary between high and mid frequency bands. Dark blue line: boundary between low and mid bands.

A Globally Normalized Neural Model for Semantic Parsing

Chenyang Huang[1], Wei Yang[2], Yanshuai Cao[2], Osmar Zaïane[1], Lili Mou[1]
[1]Department of Computing Science,
Alberta Machine Intelligence Institute (Amii), University of Alberta
[2]Borealis AI
{chenyangh, zaiane}@ualberta.ca
{wei.yang, yanshuai.cao}@borealisai.com
doublepower.mou@gmail.com

Abstract

In this paper, we propose a globally normalized model for context-free grammar (CFG)-based semantic parsing. Instead of predicting a probability, our model predicts a real-valued score at each step and does not suffer from the label bias problem. Experiments show that our approach outperforms locally normalized models on small datasets, but it does not yield improvement on a large dataset.

1 Introduction

Semantic parsing has received much interest in the NLP community (Zelle and Mooney, 1996; Zettlemoyer and Collins, 2005; Jia and Liang, 2016; Guo et al., 2020). The task is to map a natural language utterance to executable code, such as λ-expressions, SQL queries, and Python programs.

Recent work integrates the context-free grammar (CFG) of the target code into the generation process. Instead of generating tokens of the code (Dong and Lapata, 2016), CFG-based semantic parsing predicts the grammar rules in the abstract syntax tree (AST). This guarantees the generated code complies with the CFG, and thus it has been widely adopted (Yin and Neubig, 2018; Guo et al., 2019; Bogin et al., 2019; Sun et al., 2019, 2020).

Typically, the neural semantic parsing models are trained by maximum likelihood estimation (MLE). The models predict the probability of the next rules in an autoregressive fashion, known as a locally normalized model.

However, local normalization is often criticized for the label bias problem (Lafferty et al., 2001; Andor et al., 2016; Wiseman and Rush, 2016; Stanojević and Steedman, 2020). In semantic parsing, for example, grammar rules that generate identifiers (e.g., variable names) have much lower probability than other grammar rules. Thus, the model will be biased towards such rules that can avoid predicting

identifiers. More generally, the locally normalized model will prefer such early-step predictions that can lead to low entropy in future steps.

In this work, we propose to apply global normalization to neural semantic parsing. Our model scores every grammar rule with an unbounded real value, instead of a probability, so that the model does not have to avoid high-entropy predictions and does not suffer from label bias. Specifically, we use max-margin loss for training, where the ground truth is treated as the positive sample and beam search results are negative samples. In addition, we accelerate training by initializing the globally normalized model with the parameters from a pretrained locally normalized model.

We conduct experiments on three datasets: ATIS (Dahl et al., 1994), CoNaLa (Yin et al., 2018), and Spider (Yu et al., 2018). Compared with local normalization, our globally normalized model is able to achieve higher performance on the small ATIS and CoNaLa datasets with the long short-term memory (LSTM) architecture, but does not yield improvement on the massive Spider dataset when using a BERT-based pretrained language model.

2 Related Work

Early approaches to semantic parsing mainly rely on predefined templates, and are domain-specific (Zelle and Mooney, 1996; Zettlemoyer and Collins, 2005; Kwiatkowksi et al., 2010). Later, researchers apply sequence-to-sequence models to semantic parsing. Dong and Lapata (2016) propose to generate tokens along the syntax tree of a program. Yin and Neubig (2017) generate a program by predicting the grammar rules; our work uses the TranX tool (Yin and Neubig, 2018) with this framework.

Globally normalized models, such as the conditional random field (CRF, Lafferty et al., 2001), are able to mitigate the label bias problem. How-

Proceedings of the 5th Workshop on Structured Prediction for NLP, pages 61–66
August 1–6, 2021. ©2021 Association for Computational Linguistics

ever, their training is generally difficult due to the global normalization process. To tackle this challenge, Daumé and Marcu (2005) propose learning as search optimization (LaSO), and Wiseman and Rush (2016) extend it to the neural network regime as beam search optimization (BSO). Specifically, they obtain negative partial samples whenever the ground truth falls out of the beam during the search, and "restart" the beam search with the ground truth partial sequence teacher-forced.

Our work is similar to BSO. However, we search for an entire output, and do not train with partial negative samples. This is because our decoder is tree-structured, and different partial trees cannot be implemented in batch efficiently. We instead perform locally normalized pretraining to ease the training of our globally normalized model.

3   Methodology

In this section, we first introduce the neural semantic parser TranX, which servers as the locally normalized base model in our work. We then elaborate how to construct its globally normalized version.

3.1   The TranX Framework

TranX is a context-free grammar (CFG)-based neural semantic parsing system (Yin and Neubig, 2018). TranX first encodes a natural language input X with a neural network encoder.

Then, the model generates a program by predicting the grammar rules (also known as actions) along the abstract syntax tree (AST) of the program. In Figure 1, for example, the rules generating the desired program include ApplyConstr(Expr.), ApplyConstr(Call), ApplyConstr(Attr.), and GenToken(sorted).

In TranX, these actions are predicted in an autoregressive way based on the input X and the partially generated tree, given by

$$P_L(a_t|\boldsymbol{a}_{<t}, X; \boldsymbol{\theta}_L) = \frac{\exp\{o(a_t|\boldsymbol{a}_{<t}, X; \boldsymbol{\theta}_L)\}}{\sum_{a'_t \in \mathcal{A}_t(\boldsymbol{a}_{<t})} \exp\{o(a'_t|\boldsymbol{a}_{<t}, X; \boldsymbol{\theta}_L)\}}$$

(1)

where $\boldsymbol{\theta}_L$ denotes the parameters of the neural network model, and the subscript L emphasizes that the probability is locally normalized. $o(\cdot)$ denotes the logit at this step, and a_t is an action (i.e., grammar rule) among all possible actions at this step $\mathcal{A}_t(\cdot)$, which is based on previous predicted rules $\boldsymbol{a}_{<t}$.

In other words, the prediction probability is normalized at every step, and the training objective is to maximize

$$P_L(\boldsymbol{a}_{1:n}|X; \boldsymbol{\theta}_L) = \prod_{t=1}^{n} P_L(a_t|\boldsymbol{a}_{<t}, X; \boldsymbol{\theta}_L)$$

(2)

where n is the total number of steps.

3.2   Globally Normalized Training

A locally normalized model may suffer from the label bias problem (Lafferty et al., 2001). This is because such a model normalizes the probability to 1 at every step. However, the candidate action set $\mathcal{A}_t(\boldsymbol{a}_{<t})$ may have different sizes, and the actions from a smaller $\mathcal{A}_t(\boldsymbol{a}_{<t})$ typically have higher probabilities. Thus, the model would prefer such actions $\boldsymbol{a}_{<t}$ that will yield smaller $\mathcal{A}_t(\boldsymbol{a}_{<t})$ in future steps.[1]

We propose to adapt TranX to a global normalized model to alleviate label bias. Instead of predicting a probability $P(a_t|\boldsymbol{a}_{<t}, X)$ as in (2), our globally normalized model predicts a positive score at a step as

$$s(a_t|\boldsymbol{a}_{<t}, X; \boldsymbol{\theta}_G) = \exp\{o(a_t|\boldsymbol{a}_{<t}, X; \boldsymbol{\theta}_G)\} \quad (3)$$

where $o(\cdot)$ is the same logit as (1), and $\boldsymbol{\theta}_G$ is the parameters.

The probability of the sequence $\boldsymbol{a}_{1:n}$ is normalized only once in a global manner, given by

$$P_G(\boldsymbol{a}_{1:n}, X; \boldsymbol{\theta}_G) = \frac{1}{Z_G} \prod_{t=1}^{n} s(a_t|\boldsymbol{a}_{<t}, X; \boldsymbol{\theta}_G)$$

(4)

where $Z_G = \sum_{\boldsymbol{a}'_{1:n}} \prod_{t=1}^{n} s(a'_t|\boldsymbol{a}'_{<t}; \boldsymbol{\theta}_G)$ is the partition function.

A globally normalized model alleviates the label bias problem, because it does not normalize the probability at every prediction step, as seen from (4). Thus, it is not biased by the size of $\mathcal{A}_t(\boldsymbol{a}_{<t})$.

The training objective is still to maximize the likelihood, albeit normalized in a global way. However, computing the partition function Z_G requires enumerating all combinations of actions $\boldsymbol{a}'_{1:n}$ in the partition function of (4), which is generally intractable.

In practice, the maximum likelihood training is approximated by max-margin loss between a positive sample $\boldsymbol{a}_{1:n}$ and a negative sample $\boldsymbol{a}_{1:n}^{-}$,

---

[1] Or more generally, the model prefers $\mathcal{A}_t(\boldsymbol{a}_{<t})$ with a smaller entropy.

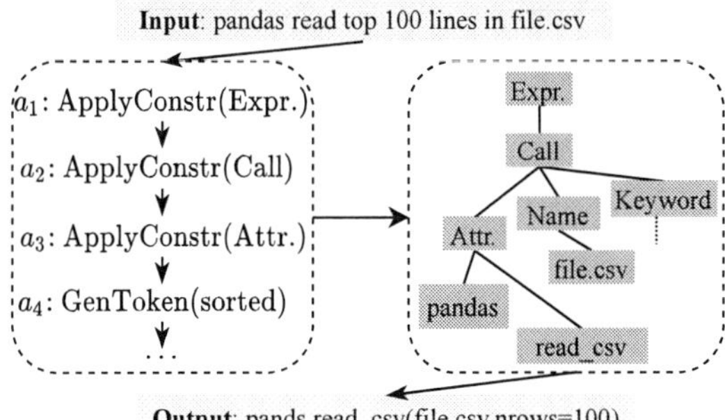

Figure 1: An example of generating a Python program with TranX.

given by

$$\mathcal{L}(\boldsymbol{a}_{1:n}^-, \boldsymbol{a}_{1:n}) = \max\{0, o(\boldsymbol{a}_{1:n}^-|X) - o(\boldsymbol{a}_{1:n}|X) + \Delta\} \tag{5}$$

where $o(\boldsymbol{a}_{1:n}|X) = \frac{1}{n}\sum_{t=1}^{n} o(a_t|\boldsymbol{a}_{<t})$ is the average of logits. Δ is a positive constant.

The positive sample is simply the ground truth actions, whereas the negative samples are obtained by beam search. In other words, we perform beam search inference during training, and the sequences in the beam (other than the ground truth) serve as the negative samples.

Similar to MLE training for (4), the max-margin loss increases the logits of the ground truth sample, while decreasing the logits for others. It is noted that the quality of negative samples will largely affect the max-margin training, as only a few samples are used to approximate Z_G.

To address this issue, we initialize the parameters of the globally normalized model $\boldsymbol{\theta}_G$ with $\boldsymbol{\theta}_L$ in a pretrained locally normalized model. Thus, our negative samples are of higher quality, so that the max-margin training is easier and more stable.

3.3 Handling the Copy Mechanism

TranX has a copy mechanism (Gu et al., 2016) as an important component for predicting the terminal nodes of the AST, as the target program largely overlaps with the source utterance, especially for entities (e.g., "file.csv" in Figure 1). In the locally normalized TranX, the copy mechanism marginalizes the probability of generating a token in the vocabulary and copying it from the source:

$$P_L(a_t = \text{GenToken}[v] \,|\, \boldsymbol{a}_{<t}, X)$$
$$= P(\text{gen} \,|\, \boldsymbol{a}_{<t}, X) P(v \,|\, \text{gen}, \boldsymbol{a}_{<t}, X)$$
$$+ P(\text{copy} \,|\, \boldsymbol{a}_{<t}, X) P(v \,|\, \text{copy}, \boldsymbol{a}_{<t}, X)$$

where GenToken[·] denotes generating a terminal token v. $P(\text{copy}|\cdot)$ is the predicted probability of copying the token v from the source utterance, and $P(\text{gen}|\cdot) = 1 - P(\text{copy}|\cdot)$ is the probability of generating v from the vocabulary.

However, the copy mechanism cannot be directly combined with global normalization, because we use unbounded, real-valued logits instead of probabilities. This would not make much sense when both logits are negative, whereas their product is positive.

Therefore, we propose a variant of copy mechanisms in the globally normalized setting. Specifically, we keep the probabilities $P(\text{copy}|\cdot)$ and $P(\text{gen}|\cdot)$, and use them to weight the logits of generating and copying a token v, given by

$$o(a_t = \text{GenToken}[v] \,|\, \boldsymbol{a}_{<t}, X)$$
$$= P(\text{gen} \,|\, \boldsymbol{a}_{<t}, X) o(v \,|\, \text{gen}, \boldsymbol{a}_{<t}, X)$$
$$+ P(\text{copy} \,|\, \boldsymbol{a}_{<t}, X) o(v \,|\, \text{copy}, \boldsymbol{a}_{<t}, X)$$

Here, $o(a_t = \text{GenToken}[v] \,|\, \cdot)$ is a linear interpolation of two logits, and thus fits the max-margin loss (5) naturally.

4 Experiments

Datasets. We conduct experiments on three benchmark parsing datasets: ATIS (Zettlemoyer and Collins, 2007), CoNaLa (Yin et al., 2018), and Spider (Yu et al., 2018), which contain 4473, 2379, and 8695 training samples, respectively.

It should be pointed out that much work adopts data anonymization techniques to replace entities with placeholders (Dong and Lapata, 2016; Yin and Neubig, 2017, 2019; Sun et al., 2020). This unfortunately causes a large number of duplicate samples between training and test. This is recently realized in Guo et al. (2020), and thus, in our work, we only compare the models using the original, correct ATIS dataset.

Settings. Our globally normalized semantic parser is developed upon the open-sourced TranX[2]. We adopt the CFG grammars provided by TranX to convert lambda calculus and Python programs into ASTs and sequence of grammar rules (actions). For ATIS and CoNaLa datasets, we use long LSTM models as both the encoder and the decoder. Their dimensions are set to 256. For the Spider dataset, we use a pretrained BERT model[3] (Devlin et al.,

---

[2]https://github.com/pcyin/tranX

[3]Specifically, we use the RoBERTa-base model (Liu et al., 2019) as we find it performs better than the original BERT-base model (Devlin et al., 2019).

	Dev	Test
Jia and Liang (2016)		
No copy	N/A	69.90%
Copy	N/A	76.30%
Copy + data recombination	N/A	**83.30%**
Guo et al. (2020)		
No copy	N/A	68.70%
Copy	N/A	75.70%
Ours		
No copy	80.00%	71.49%
Copy	79.15%	75.63%
Copy + global	81.61%	76.32%
Copy + global + emb	**84.53%**	**78.16%**

Table 1: Exact match accuracy on the ATIS dataset.

	Dev	Test
Yin and Neubig (2018)	N/A	24.35%
+ Reranking	N/A	30.11%
Ours (local)	33.46%	25.84%
+ Reranking	**35.82%**	**28.39%**
+ Global	34.75%	27.08%

Table 2: BLEU score on the CoNaLa dataset.

	Dev Acc.
Rubin and Berant (2020)	73.4%
Yu et al. (2021)	74.7%
Ours (local)	73.79%
+ Global	73.69%

Table 3: Exact match accuracy on the Spider dataset. Test performance requires submissions to the official website. We report validation performance instead.

2019) and the relation-aware Transformer (Wang et al., 2020) as the encoder and an LSTM as the decoder. The architecture generally follows the work by Xu et al. (2021).

The beam size is set to 20 to search for negative samples, and is set to 5 for inference. The margin Δ in (5) is set to 0.1. We use the Adam optimizer (Kingma and Ba, 2015) with a learning rate of 5e-4 for training.

For both ATIS and CoNaLa datasets, we report the best results on the development sets and the corresponding results on the test set. For the Spider dataset, we only report the results on the development set as the ground truth of the test set is not publicly available.

5 Results

ATIS dataset. Following Yin and Neubig (2017); Sun et al. (2020), we report the exact match accuracy for ATIS. We first replicate locally normalized models with and without the copy mechanism and achieve similar results to Jia and Liang (2016) and Guo et al. (2020), shown in Table 1. This verifies that we have a fair implementation and are ready for the study of global normalization.

We observe that the copy mechanism largely affects the accuracy on the test set, although it has little effect on the development set. This is because the training and validation distributions closely resemble each other, whereas the test distribution differs largely. Therefore, the copy mechanism is important for handling unseen entities in the test set, and our proposed copy variant in Section 3.3 is also essential to globally normalized models.

We then train our model with the max-margin loss. Our globally normalized model consistently improves the accuracy on both development and test sets, compared with its locally normalized counterpart. This shows the effectiveness of our approach.

In addition, we notice that a large number of entities in ATIS have a form like "ap:denvor" (Denver Airport). We thus use the combination of character-level ELMo embeddings (Peters et al., 2018) and word-level GloVe embeddings (Pennington et al., 2014). This further improves the accuracy, which outperforms the previous methods by $\sim 1.9\%$ in the setting without data augmentation.

CoNaLa dataset. For CoNaLa, BLEU is treated as the main metric in previous work (Yin and Neubig, 2019), because accuracy is generally very low (<3%) on this dataset. From Table 2, we observe that our globally normalized model improves the BLEU scores on both the development and test sets compared with the locally normalized baseline. Such improvement is consistent with that on ATIS.

We further compare our model with Yin and Neubig (2019), which reranks beam search results by heuristics. Our method is outperformed by the reranking approach. Note that reranking can be considered as alleviating label bias with postprocessing, as the locally normalized model fails to assign the correct sequence with the highest joint probability. However, the reranking method requires training several reranking scorers, combined with an ad hoc feature (namely, length). By contrast, our global normalization does not rely on ad hoc human engineering.

Spider dataset. Table 3 lists the results on the Spider dataset. Here, our locally normalized model uses BERT as the encoder, and its performance is on par with that from the recent state-of-the-art approaches (Rubin and Berant, 2020; Yu et al., 2021). However, our global normalization does not improve the performance. It is noted that BERT is a more powerful model than LSTM, and Spider has a much larger training set than CoNaLa and ATIS. We conjuncture that BERT learns the step-by-step local prediction probability very well, which in turn yields a satisfying joint probability and largely mitigates label bias by itself. Therefore, the globally normalized model does not exhibit its superiority on the Spider dataset.

6 Conclusion

In this work, we propose to apply global normalization for neural semantic parsing. Our approach predicts the score of different grammar rules at an autoregressive step, and thus it does not suffer from the label bias problem. We observe that our proposed method is able to improve performance on small datasets with LSTM-based encoders. However, global normalization becomes less effective on the large dataset with a BERT architecture.

Acknowledgments

We acknowledge the support of the Mitacs Accelerate Program (Ref: IT16065) and the Natural Sciences and Engineering Research Council of Canada (NSERC) under grant Nos. RGPIN-2020-04465 and RGPIN-2020-04440. Chenyang Huang is supported by the Borealis AI Graduate Fellowship Program. Lili Mou and Osmar Zaïane are supported by the Amii Fellow Program and the Canada CIFAR AI Chair Program. This research is also supported in part by Compute Canada (www.computecanada.ca).

References

Daniel Andor, Chris Alberti, David Weiss, Aliaksei Severyn, Alessandro Presta, Kuzman Ganchev, Slav Petrov, and Michael Collins. 2016. Globally normalized transition-based neural networks. In *Proceedings of the 54th Annual Meeting of the Association for Computational Linguistics*, pages 2442–2452.

Ben Bogin, Jonathan Berant, and Matt Gardner. 2019. Representing schema structure with graph neural networks for text-to-SQL parsing. In *Proceedings of the 57th Annual Meeting of the Association for Computational Linguistics*, pages 4560–4565.

Deborah A. Dahl, Madeleine Bates, Michael Brown, William Fisher, Kate Hunicke-Smith, David Pallett, Christine Pao, Alexander Rudnicky, and Elizabeth Shriberg. 1994. Expanding the scope of the ATIS task: The ATIS-3 corpus. In *Human Language Technology: Proceedings of a Workshop held at Plainsboro, New Jersey, March 8-11, 1994*.

Hal Daumé and Daniel Marcu. 2005. Learning as search optimization: Approximate large margin methods for structured prediction. In *Proceedings of the 22nd International Conference on Machine Learning*, pages 169–176.

Jacob Devlin, Ming-Wei Chang, Kenton Lee, and Kristina Toutanova. 2019. BERT: Pre-training of deep bidirectional transformers for language understanding. In *Proceedings of the 2019 Conference of the North American Chapter of the Association for Computational Linguistics: Human Language Technologies*, pages 4171–4186.

Li Dong and Mirella Lapata. 2016. Language to logical form with neural attention. In *Proceedings of the 54th Annual Meeting of the Association for Computational Linguistics*, pages 33–43.

Jiatao Gu, Zhengdong Lu, Hang Li, and Victor O.K. Li. 2016. Incorporating copying mechanism in sequence-to-sequence learning. In *Proceedings of the 54th Annual Meeting of the Association for Computational Linguistics*, pages 1631–1640.

Jiaqi Guo, Qian Liu, Jian-Guang Lou, Zhenwen Li, Xueqing Liu, Tao Xie, and Ting Liu. 2020. Benchmarking meaning representations in neural semantic parsing. In *Proceedings of the Conference on Empirical Methods in Natural Language Processing*, pages 1520–1540.

Jiaqi Guo, Zecheng Zhan, Yan Gao, Yan Xiao, Jian-Guang Lou, Ting Liu, and Dongmei Zhang. 2019. Towards complex text-to-SQL in crossdomain database with intermediate representation. In *Proceedings of the 57th Annual Meeting of the Association for Computational Linguistics*, pages 4524–4535.

Robin Jia and Percy Liang. 2016. Data recombination for neural semantic parsing. In *Proceedings of the 54th Annual Meeting of the Association for Computational Linguistics*, pages 12–22.

Diederik P. Kingma and Jimmy Ba. 2015. Adam: A method for stochastic optimization. In *International Conference on Learning Representations*.

Tom Kwiatkowksi, Luke Zettlemoyer, Sharon Goldwater, and Mark Steedman. 2010. Inducing probabilistic CCG grammars from logical form with higher-order unification. In *Proceedings of the 2010 Conference on Empirical Methods in Natural Language Processing*, pages 1223–1233.

John D. Lafferty, Andrew McCallum, and Fernando C. N. Pereira. 2001. Conditional random fields: Probabilistic models for segmenting and labeling sequence data. In *Proceedings of the Eighteenth International Conference on Machine Learning*, pages 282–289.

Yinhan Liu, Myle Ott, Naman Goyal, Jingfei Du, Mandar Joshi, Danqi Chen, Omer Levy, Mike Lewis, Luke Zettlemoyer, and Veselin Stoyanov. 2019. RoBERTa: A robustly optimized bert pretraining approach. *arXiv preprint arXiv:1907.11692*.

Jeffrey Pennington, Richard Socher, and Christopher Manning. 2014. GloVe: Global vectors for word representation. In *Proceedings of the 2014 Conference on Empirical Methods in Natural Language Processing*, pages 1532–1543.

Matthew Peters, Mark Neumann, Mohit Iyyer, Matt Gardner, Christopher Clark, Kenton Lee, and Luke Zettlemoyer. 2018. Deep contextualized word representations. In *Proceedings of the 2018 Conference of the North American Chapter of the Association for Computational Linguistics: Human Language Technologies*, pages 2227–2237.

Ohad Rubin and Jonathan Berant. 2020. SmBoP: Semi-autoregressive bottom-up semantic parsing. *arXiv preprint arXiv:2010.12412*.

Miloš Stanojević and Mark Steedman. 2020. Max-margin incremental CCG parsing. In *Proceedings of the 58th Annual Meeting of the Association for Computational Linguistics*, pages 4111–4122.

Zeyu Sun, Qihao Zhu, Lili Mou, Yingfei Xiong, Ge Li, and Lu Zhang. 2019. A grammar-based structural cnn decoder for code generation. In *Proceedings of the AAAI Conference on Artificial Intelligence*, pages 7055–7062.

Zeyu Sun, Qihao Zhu, Yingfei Xiong, Yican Sun, Lili Mou, and Lu Zhang. 2020. TreeGen: A tree-based transformer architecture for code generation. In *Proceedings of the Thirty-Fourth AAAI Conference on Artificial Intelligence*, pages 8984–8991.

Bailin Wang, Richard Shin, Xiaodong Liu, Oleksandr Polozov, and Matthew Richardson. 2020. RAT-SQL: Relation-aware schema encoding and linking for text-to-SQL parsers. In *Proceedings of the 58th Annual Meeting of the Association for Computational Linguistics*, pages 7567–7578.

Sam Wiseman and Alexander M. Rush. 2016. Sequence-to-sequence learning as beam-search optimization. In *Proceedings of the 2016 Conference on Empirical Methods in Natural Language Processing*, pages 1296–1306.

Peng Xu, Dhruv Kumar, Wei Yang, Wenjie Zi, Keyi Tang, Chenyang Huang, Jackie Chi Kit Cheung, Simon JD Prince, and Yanshuai Cao. 2021. Optimizing deeper transformers on small datasets. *arXiv preprint arXiv:2012.15355*.

Pengcheng Yin, Bowen Deng, Edgar Chen, Bogdan Vasilescu, and Graham Neubig. 2018. Learning to mine aligned code and natural language pairs from stack overflow. In *Proceedings of the International Conference on Mining Software Repositories*, pages 476–486.

Pengcheng Yin and Graham Neubig. 2017. A syntactic neural model for general-purpose code generation. In *Proceedings of the 55th Annual Meeting of the Association for Computational Linguistics*, pages 440–450.

Pengcheng Yin and Graham Neubig. 2018. TRANX: A transition-based neural abstract syntax parser for semantic parsing and code generation. In *Proceedings of the 2018 Conference on Empirical Methods in Natural Language Processing: System Demonstrations*, pages 7–12.

Pengcheng Yin and Graham Neubig. 2019. Reranking for neural semantic parsing. In *Proceedings of the 57th Annual Meeting of the Association for Computational Linguistics*, pages 4553–4559.

Tao Yu, Chien-Sheng Wu, Xi Victoria Lin, bailin wang, Yi Chern Tan, Xinyi Yang, Dragomir Radev, richard socher, and Caiming Xiong. 2021. GraPPa: Grammar-augmented pre-training for table semantic parsing. In *The International Conference on Learning Representations*.

Tao Yu, Rui Zhang, Kai Yang, Michihiro Yasunaga, Dongxu Wang, Zifan Li, James Ma, Irene Li, Qingning Yao, Shanelle Roman, Zilin Zhang, and Dragomir Radev. 2018. Spider: A large-scale human-labeled dataset for complex and cross-domain semantic parsing and text-to-SQL task. In *Proceedings of the Conference on Empirical Methods in Natural Language Processing*, pages 3911–3921.

John M. Zelle and Raymond J. Mooney. 1996. Learning to parse database queries using inductive logic programming. In *Proceedings of the Thirteenth National Conference on Artificial Intelligence*, pages 1050–1055.

Luke Zettlemoyer and Michael Collins. 2007. Online learning of relaxed CCG grammars for parsing to logical form. In *Proceedings of the Joint Conference on Empirical Methods in Natural Language Processing and Computational Natural Language Learning*, pages 678–687.

Luke S. Zettlemoyer and Michael Collins. 2005. Learning to map sentences to logical form: Structured classification with probabilistic categorial grammars. In *Proceedings of the Twenty-First Conference on Uncertainty in Artificial Intelligence*, pages 658–666.

Comparing Span Extraction Methods for Semantic Role Labeling

Zhisong Zhang, Emma Strubell, Eduard Hovy
Language Technologies Institute, Carnegie Mellon University
zhisongz@cs.cmu.edu, strubell@cmu.edu, hovy@cmu.edu

Abstract

In this work, we empirically compare span
extraction methods for the task of semantic
role labeling (SRL). While recent progress
incorporating pre-trained contextualized representations into neural encoders has greatly
improved SRL F1 performance on popular
benchmarks, the potential costs and benefits
of structured decoding in these models have
become less clear. With extensive experiments on PropBank SRL datasets, we find
that more structured decoding methods out-
perform BIO-tagging when using static (word
type) embeddings across all experimental settings. However, when used in conjunction
with pre-trained contextualized word representations, the benefits are diminished. We also
experiment in cross-genre and cross-lingual
settings and find similar trends. We further perform speed comparisons and provide analysis
on the accuracy-efficiency trade-offs among
different decoding methods.

1 Introduction

Semantic role labeling (SRL) is a core natural language processing (NLP) task that aims to identify
predicate-argument structures in text (Gildea and
Jurafsky, 2002; Palmer et al., 2010). Following
the neural encoder-decoder paradigm, we can view
an SRL model as combining an encoder, which
builds hidden representations for the input words,
with a decoder, which extracts the argument spans
based on the encoded representations. While recent
SRL models achieve high performance on popular
benchmarks (Zhou and Xu, 2015; He et al., 2017;
Tan et al., 2018; Strubell et al., 2018; Shi and Lin,
2019), most improvements come from better neural encoders, such as the Transformer (Vaswani
et al., 2017) and pre-trained contextualized word
representations, such as BERT (Devlin et al., 2019).
However, influence on end-task performance due
to the choice of decoder has become less clear.

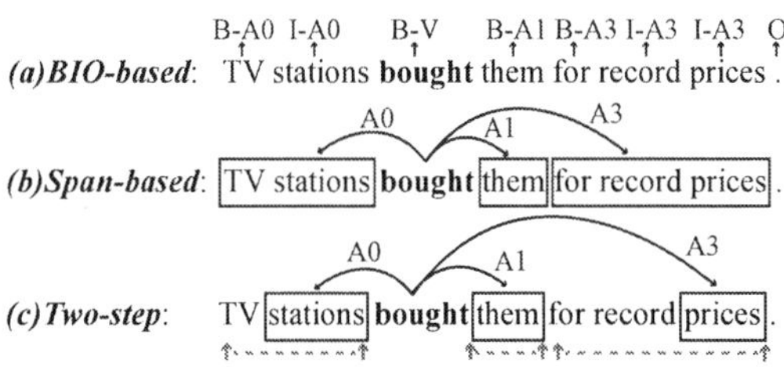

Figure 1: Illustration of decoding methods explored
in this work. For the predicate **"bought"**, we identify argument spans by: (a) BIO-based sequence labeling; (b) direct span-based extraction; (c) two-step approach: first identifying head words, then expanding to
full spans by deciding left and right boundaries.

In this work, we perform an empirical investiga-
tion of different decoding methods for span extraction, as illustrated in Figure 1. The most common
strategy casts the task as a sequence labeling problem using the BIO-tagging scheme (Zhou and Xu,
2015; He et al., 2017; Tan et al., 2018; Strubell
et al., 2018; Shi and Lin, 2019). While this approach is simple, it does not directly model the
arguments at the span level. Alternatively, the span-
based method directly builds representations for all
possible[1] spans and selects among them (He et al.,
2018a; Ouchi et al., 2018). Though this approach is
straightforward for explicitly modeling span-level
information, composing a representation for every
span can lead to higher computational cost. Inspired by dependency-based SRL (Surdeanu et al.,
2008; Hajič et al., 2009), a third option first identifies a head word then decides the span boundaries.
This two-step strategy has been explored in previous work on information extraction (Peng et al.,
2015; Lin et al., 2019; Zhang et al., 2020), and we
apply it here to SRL. Compared with the sequential
BIO-tagger, the latter two approaches more directly
model the argument span structures; we thus refer

---

[1] Up to a fixed length, decided as a hyperparameter.

Proceedings of the 5th Workshop on Structured Prediction for NLP, pages 67–77
August 1–6, 2021. ©2021 Association for Computational Linguistics

to them as more *structured* decoders.

We perform careful comparisons of these decoding methods upon the same encoding backbone, based on a deep Transformer encoder. We first experiment in the standard fully-supervised settings on English PropBank datasets (CoNLL-2005 and CoNLL-2012). The results show that more structured decoders, especially the two-step approach with syntactic guidance, consistently perform better than BIO-tagging when using static word embeddings. However, if including strong contextualized BERT embeddings, the benefits of more structured decoding are diminished and the simplest BIO-tagging method performs well across different experimental settings. Error analysis shows that contextualized embeddings help in deciding span boundaries. Furthermore, we explore cross-genre and cross-lingual settings on the CoNLL-2012 datasets, and find similar trends. Finally, we perform speed comparisons and analyze the accuracy-efficiency trade-offs among different decoding methods.

2 Model

For a given predicate,[2] SRL aims to extract all argument spans and assign them role labels. To model this task, we follow the neural encoder-decoder paradigm: the encoder produces hidden representations for the input words, upon which the decoder decides the structured outputs. All our models adopt the same encoding architecture: a deep Transformer encoder (Vaswani et al., 2017), which has been shown effective for SRL (Tan et al., 2018; Strubell et al., 2018). For a given input sequence of words $\{w_1, \ldots, w_n\}$, we obtain their contextualized representations $\{h_1, \ldots, h_n\}$ from the encoder. Upon these, we stack different decoders to extract the argument spans corresponding to different extraction strategies, which will be described in the following.

2.1 BIO-based

Since argument spans do not overlap in the datasets we explore, the BIO-tagging scheme (Ramshaw and Marcus, 1999) can be utilized to extract them, casting SRL as a sequence labeling problem.

For each word, we feed its representation h to a multi-layer perceptron (MLP) based scorer, which assigns the scores of the BIO tags. Assuming that

we have k possible argument roles in the output space, each of them will have its "B-" and "I-" tags. Together with the "O" (NIL) tag, the tagging space has a dimension of $2k + 1$.

Furthermore, we consider the option of adopting a standard linear-chain conditional random field (CRF; Lafferty et al., 2001) to model pairwise tagging transitions. If adopting the CRF (BIO w/ CRF), we train the model with sequence-level negative log likelihood and use the Viterbi algorithm for inference. If not using the CRF (BIO w/o CRF), we simply use tag-level cross entropy as the learning objective and perform argmax greedy decoding at inference time, following Tan et al. (2018).

2.2 Span-based

In the span-based method, we build neural representations for all candidate spans and directly select and assign role labels (or NIL). Following He et al. (2018a), for a span a, we compose its representation from start and end points, soft head-word vectors and span width features by concatenation:

$$\mathbf{g}(a) = [h_{start(a)}, h_{end(a)}, \text{soft}(a), \text{width}(a)]$$

Here, $\text{soft}(a)$ denotes a soft-head representation obtained from an attention mechanism:

$$\text{soft}(a) = \sum_{start(a) \leq i \leq end(a)} \text{att}(i, a) h_i$$

$$\text{att}(i, a) = \frac{w_{att}^T h_i}{\sum_{start(a) \leq i' \leq end(a)} w_{att}^T h_{i'}}$$

and $\text{width}(a)$ denotes a width embedding corresponding to the span size (width).

All valid candidate spans are first assigned an unlabeled score, using an MLP scorer. This unary score is then used as the criterion for beam pruning to reduce the computational costs of full labeling. Since each predicate will not have too many arguments (most have less than 5), we adopt a fixed beam size of 10. We also limit the maximum width of candidate spans to 30, which covers around 99% of the cases. Surviving candidates are further assigned label scores with another MLP scorer, with which we decide output arguments.

2.3 Two-step

In this approach, we decompose the problem into two steps: head-selection and boundary-decision. In the first step, each individual word is directly scored for argument labels (or NIL). We again adopt an MLP classifier to obtain the probability

---

[2]In this work, we focus on argument extraction and assume given predicates.

that a word can be the head of an argument with label r (r can be NIL). The non-NIL labeled words are selected as the head words of the arguments. Since the annotations usually do not contain head words for the argument spans, we further consider two strategies to provide supervision for training:

HeadSyntax A straightforward method is to adopt guidance from syntax. Following dependency-style SRL (Surdeanu et al., 2008; Hajič et al., 2009), we use syntactic dependency parse trees and select the highest word (the one that is closest to the root) in the span as the head. In training, we only assign the argument role to the syntactic head word, and all other words in the span get a label of NIL.

HeadAuto In this strategy, all words in an argument span can be considered as the potential head word. We adopt the *bag loss* from Lin et al. (2019) to train the model to automatically identify head words. Specifically, for a word w_i inside an argument span a which has the role r, the loss is computed as:

$$\text{Loss}(w_i) = \delta_i \cdot [-\log p(r|h_i)]$$
$$+ (1 - \delta_i) \cdot [-\log p(\text{NIL}|h_i)]$$
$$\delta_i = \frac{p(r|h_i)}{\max_{start(a) \leq j \leq end(a)} p(r|h_j)}$$

Here, words that are more indicative for the argument will be assigned higher probabilities to the argument role. This will give them larger loss weights (δ) and thus further encourage them to be the heads. In this way, the head words are decided automatically by the model.

In the second step, we determine span boundaries for these head words. Here we adopt the span selection method from extractive question answering (Wang and Jiang, 2016; Devlin et al., 2019) using two classifiers to decide the start and end words ($[s, e]$) of a span:

$$p(s, e) = p_{start}(s) \cdot p_{end}(e)$$
$$p_{start}(s) = \frac{\exp \text{score}_{start}(h'_s)}{\sum_i \exp \text{score}_{start}(h'_i)}$$
$$p_{end}(e) = \frac{\exp \text{score}_{end}(h'_e)}{\sum_i \exp \text{score}_{end}(h'_i)}$$

Here, we first add indicator embeddings to the head word's encoder representations to mark its positions, and then stack one self-attention layer to obtain head-word-aware representations for the in-

put sequence: $\{h'_1, \cdots, h'_n\}$. We further introduce two linear scorers to assign the start and end scores for each word, which are further normalized across the input sequence. For training, the objective is minimizing the sum of negative log-likelihoods of picking the correct start and end positions. When decoding, we select the maximum scoring span whose boundaries s and e satisfy $s \leq e$.

We observe that at inference time, sometimes different head words may expand to overlapping spans, which do not appear in the datasets we explore. To deal with this, we adopt a greedy post-processing procedure to remove overlapping argument spans: iterating through all argument spans ranked by model score and only keeping the ones that do not overlap with previous surviving ones.

3 Experiments

3.1 Settings

Data The models are evaluated on standard Prop-Bank datasets from the CoNLL-2005 shared task (Carreras and Màrquez, 2005) and the CoNLL-2012 subset of OntoNotes 5.0 (Pradhan et al., 2013). Table 1 lists the relevant statistics. For CoNLL-2005, we follow the splits from the CoNLL-2005 shared task.[3] For the English part of CoNLL-2012, we adopt the data from Pradhan et al. (2013)[4] but follow the splits of the CoNLL-2012 shared task.[5] For the Chinese part of CoNLL-2012, we directly utilize those provided by the CoNLL-2012 shared task. For evaluation, we adopt the standard evaluation script of `srl-eval.pl`.[6] For the "HeadSyntax" method that requires dependency trees, we convert the original constituencies to Universal Dependencies (Nivre et al., 2020) using Stanford CoreNLP (Manning et al., 2014) version 4.1.0. Notice that we only need syntactic information to be provided during training, since the model predicts head words itself at test time.

Input Features and Encoder For fair comparison, we adopt the same input features, deep Transformer-based encoders and training schemes across all experiments. We consider two types of word features: static word embeddings and

---

[3]https://www.cs.upc.edu/~srlconll/
[4]https://cemantix.org/data/ontonotes.html
[5]https://conll.cemantix.org/2012/
[6]https://www.cs.upc.edu/~srlconll/soft.html

	CoNLL 2005				CoNLL 2012 (English)			CoNLL 2012 (Chinese)		
	Train	Dev	Test	Brown	Train	Dev	Test	Train	Dev	Test
Sent.	39.8k	1.3k	2.4k	0.4k	75.2k	9.6k	9.5k	36.5k	6.1k	4.5k
Pred.	90.8k	3.2k	5.3k	0.8k	188.9k	23.9k	24.5k	117.1k	16.6k	15.0k
Arg.	333.7k	11.7k	19.6k	3.0k	622.5k	78.1k	80.2k	365.3k	51.0k	46.7k

Table 1: Statistics of the datasets: Number of sentences (Sent.), predicates (Pred.) and arguments (Arg.).

pre-trained contextualized embeddings[7] from BERT$_{base}$. In the English experiments, we adopt fastText[8] embeddings (Mikolov et al., 2018) and frozen features from `bert-base-cased`. In the cross-lingual experiments, we only utilize multi-lingual BERT features from `bert-base-multilingual-cased`. Before feeding the word-level features to the encoder, we concatenate them and apply a linear layer to project them to the encoding dimension. We further add indicator embeddings to let the model be aware of the positions of the predicates. For both cases of static embedding and BERT features, we adopt a 10-layer Transformer module as the encoder. The head number, model dimension and feed-forward dimension are set to 8, 512 and 1024, respectively. In addition, we adopt relative positional encodings for the Transformer (Shaw et al., 2018) since we found slightly better performance in preliminary experiments.

Training We use the Adam optimizer (Kingma and Ba, 2014) for training. The learning rate is linearly increased towards 2e-4 within the first 8k steps as warm up. After this, we decay the learning rate by 0.75 each time the performance on the development set does not increase for 10 checkpoints. We train the model for a maximum of 150k steps and do validation every 1k steps to select the best model. One model contains around 40M parameters (excluding BERT). For each update, the batch size is around 4096 tokens. We apply dropout rates of 0.2 to the hidden layers. For models using static embeddings, we further replace input words by a special UNK token with a probability of 0.5 if it appears less than 3 times in the training set. At test time, a word is represented by UNK if it is not found in the collection of static word embeddings. All the experiments are run with our own

Model	WSJ	Brown	OntoNotes
He et al. (2018a)	87.4	80.4	85.5
Ouchi et al. (2018)	87.6	78.7	86.2
Shi and Lin (2019)	**88.8**	82.0	86.5
Ours (BIO w/ CRF)	87.9	**82.1**	**86.6**

Table 2: Comparisons of F1 scores with previous work in the fully-supervised settings (with single model).

implementation[9]. All the models are trained and evaluated on one TITAN-RTX GPU, and training one model takes around 1 day in our environment.

3.2 Fully-supervised Experiments

We first experiment in the fully-supervised settings on English data. Table 2 lists the comparisons of our test results (BIO w/ CRF using BERT features) to previous work. Generally our model can obtain comparable results, which verifies the quality of our implementation.

Tables 3 and 4 list our main comparisons on the development and test sets. The overall trends are very similar. For BIO-tagging, incorporating a structured CRF layer is generally helpful, which can improve the F1 scores by around 0.5 points. When not using BERT features, more structured decoders generally perform better than BIO-tagging. With the head word oracles from the syntax trees, "HeadSyntax" performs the best overall. This agrees with Strubell et al. (2018) and Swayamdipta et al. (2018), showing the helpfulness of syntactic information for SRL. However, when utilizing BERT features, the benefits of more structured decoders are diminished and the simple BIO-tagger robustly performs well. It seems that with a powerful encoder, the choice of the decoder plays a smaller role for final performance.

To further investigate this phenomenon, we perform error analysis on the development outputs of "BIO (w/ CRF)" and "HeadSyntax," which are the two that perform the best overall. We group the errors into four categories: "Boundary" denotes that the predicted head words and role labels match

---

[7]We concatenate layer 7, 8 and 9 of BERT hidden representations. For words that are split into sub-tokens, we utilize the representations of the first sub-token.

[8]`https://fasttext.cc/docs/en/english-vectors.html`

[9]`https://github.com/zzsfornlp/zmsp/`

	CoNLL2005 In-domain (WSJ)			CoNLL 2012 (OntoNotes)		
	P	R	F1	P	R	F1
Without BERT						
BIO (w/o CRF)	83.11	83.89	$83.49_{\pm0.20}$	81.43	82.75	$82.09_{\pm0.22}$
BIO (w/ CRF)	83.66	84.27	$83.96_{\pm0.26}$	82.41	**83.77**	$83.09_{\pm0.11}$
Span	84.60	83.57	$84.08_{\pm0.23}$	82.89	83.04	$82.96_{\pm0.12}$
HeadSyntax	**84.81**	**84.48**	$\mathbf{84.65}_{\pm0.18}$	**83.12**	83.42	$\mathbf{83.27}_{\pm0.18}$
HeadAuto	84.52	84.38	$84.45_{\pm0.22}$	82.50	83.16	$82.83_{\pm0.15}$
With BERT						
BIO (w/o CRF)	86.47	87.50	$86.98_{\pm0.12}$	85.22	86.94	$86.08_{\pm0.15}$
BIO (w/ CRF)	86.78	**87.84**	$87.31_{\pm0.13}$	85.66	**87.19**	$\mathbf{86.42}_{\pm0.12}$
Span	86.94	86.76	$86.85_{\pm0.16}$	85.83	86.37	$86.10_{\pm0.11}$
HeadSyntax	**87.35**	87.48	$\mathbf{87.41}_{\pm0.14}$	**86.04**	86.79	$86.41_{\pm0.12}$
HeadAuto	87.10	87.67	$87.38_{\pm0.22}$	85.80	86.75	$86.27_{\pm0.15}$

Table 3: Development results for the fully-supervised experiments. All the numbers are averaged over 5 runs with different random seeds, standard deviations of F1 scores are also reported.

	CoNLL 2005 In-domain (WSJ)			Out-of-domain (Brown)			CoNLL 2012 (OntoNotes)		
	P	R	F1	P	R	F1	P	R	F1
Without BERT									
BIO (w/o CRF)	84.42	84.94	$84.68_{\pm0.25}$	73.56	73.03	$73.29_{\pm0.43}$	81.74	82.98	$82.35_{\pm0.24}$
BIO (w/ CRF)	85.04	85.35	$85.20_{\pm0.12}$	74.25	73.92	$74.08_{\pm0.31}$	82.79	**84.11**	$83.44_{\pm0.21}$
Span	85.68	84.62	$85.14_{\pm0.32}$	75.88	74.23	$75.05_{\pm0.42}$	83.42	83.49	$83.46_{\pm0.15}$
HeadSyntax	**85.84**	**85.38**	$\mathbf{85.61}_{\pm0.11}$	**75.92**	**74.74**	$\mathbf{75.33}_{\pm0.58}$	**83.55**	83.82	$\mathbf{83.68}_{\pm0.11}$
HeadAuto	85.30	85.17	$85.23_{\pm0.14}$	74.98	73.85	$74.41_{\pm0.50}$	83.09	83.71	$83.40_{\pm0.09}$
With BERT									
BIO (w/o CRF)	87.21	87.95	$87.58_{\pm0.28}$	81.26	81.79	$81.52_{\pm0.23}$	85.33	86.97	$86.14_{\pm0.10}$
BIO (w/ CRF)	87.54	**88.32**	$\mathbf{87.93}_{\pm0.16}$	81.91	**82.37**	$\mathbf{82.14}_{\pm0.20}$	85.93	**87.32**	$\mathbf{86.62}_{\pm0.14}$
Span	87.75	87.33	$87.54_{\pm0.14}$	81.87	81.60	$81.73_{\pm0.77}$	85.97	86.26	$86.12_{\pm0.09}$
HeadSyntax	**87.76**	87.96	$87.86_{\pm0.08}$	**82.10**	81.60	$81.85_{\pm0.90}$	**86.17**	86.77	$\mathbf{86.47}_{\pm0.10}$
HeadAuto	87.70	88.15	$\mathbf{87.93}_{\pm0.12}$	81.52	81.36	$81.44_{\pm0.37}$	86.00	86.84	$86.42_{\pm0.09}$

Table 4: Test results of the fully-supervised experiments. All the results are averaged over five runs with different random seeds, standard deviations of the F1 scores are also reported.

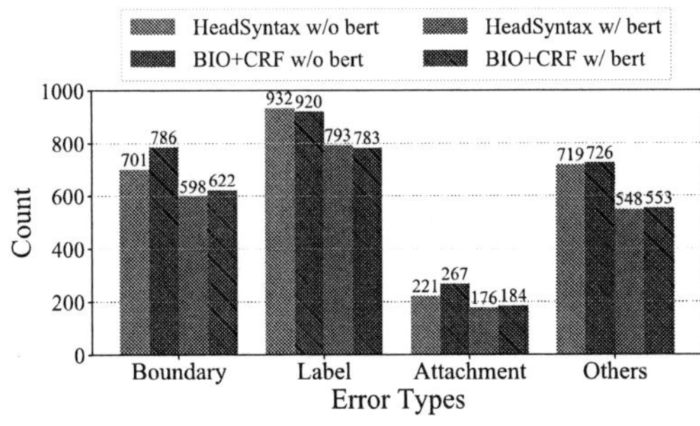

Figure 2: Error breakdown for "BIO" and "HeadSyntax" on the CoNLL-2005 development set.

the gold ones but the span boundaries are incorrect; "Label" denotes that the predicted spans are correct but the role labels are wrong; "Attachment" denotes the errors caused by incorrect phrase attachments, while "Others" denotes the remaining errors, which are other missing and over-predicted arguments. The results are shown in Figure 2. When not using BERT features, the main advantages of "HeadSyntax" over "BIO" are on the "Boundary" and "Attachment" errors, where the former makes 11% fewer "Boundary" and 17% fewer "Attachment" errors. Notice that these two types of errors are closely related to syntax, and they are mainly caused by incorrect phrase boundary predictions. In this way, it seems natural that incorporating syntactic information with head words can be helpful in this scenario. Nevertheless, when utilizing BERT features, these advantages are reduced to a negligible level. This indicates that BERT may provide sufficient information overlapping with syntax to help on boundary decisions.

3.3 Cross-genre Experiments

We further explore English cross-genre settings. We utilize English CoNLL-2012 subsets of

	nw*	bc	bn	mz	pt	tc	wb	Avg.
Without BERT								
BIO (w/o CRF)	$77.51_{\pm0.17}$	$59.91_{\pm0.31}$	$73.28_{\pm0.62}$	$71.15_{\pm0.37}$	$81.03_{\pm0.31}$	$67.90_{\pm0.37}$	$72.36_{\pm0.07}$	71.88
BIO (w/ CRF)	$78.42_{\pm0.39}$	$60.15_{\pm0.40}$	$73.97_{\pm0.15}$	$71.37_{\pm0.13}$	$81.51_{\pm0.36}$	$68.72_{\pm0.34}$	$72.54_{\pm0.41}$	72.38
Span	$79.08_{\pm0.16}$	$62.74_{\pm0.49}$	$74.80_{\pm0.30}$	$72.77_{\pm0.36}$	$\mathbf{82.42}_{\pm0.41}$	$68.93_{\pm0.12}$	$74.17_{\pm0.15}$	73.56
HeadSyntax	$\mathbf{79.54}_{\pm0.37}$	$\mathbf{62.81}_{\pm0.58}$	$\mathbf{75.06}_{\pm0.25}$	$\mathbf{73.17}_{\pm0.32}$	$82.10_{\pm0.30}$	$68.74_{\pm0.54}$	$\mathbf{74.82}_{\pm0.19}$	**73.75**
HeadAuto	$79.04_{\pm0.22}$	$61.97_{\pm0.30}$	$74.09_{\pm0.25}$	$72.56_{\pm0.40}$	$81.80_{\pm0.40}$	$\mathbf{69.25}_{\pm0.39}$	$73.96_{\pm0.19}$	73.24
With BERT								
BIO (w/o CRF)	$83.55_{\pm0.24}$	$73.37_{\pm0.51}$	$80.02_{\pm0.19}$	$78.45_{\pm0.34}$	$87.63_{\pm0.19}$	$74.89_{\pm0.41}$	$79.49_{\pm0.29}$	79.63
BIO (w/ CRF)	$83.73_{\pm0.28}$	$75.24_{\pm0.89}$	$80.64_{\pm0.15}$	$78.75_{\pm0.56}$	$\mathbf{87.94}_{\pm0.42}$	$75.38_{\pm0.42}$	$79.66_{\pm0.39}$	80.19
Span	$83.41_{\pm0.18}$	$74.22_{\pm0.89}$	$80.85_{\pm0.29}$	$78.69_{\pm0.39}$	$87.44_{\pm0.16}$	$75.05_{\pm0.36}$	$79.44_{\pm0.33}$	79.87
HeadSyntax	$\mathbf{83.96}_{\pm0.34}$	$\mathbf{75.98}_{\pm0.94}$	$\mathbf{80.88}_{\pm0.17}$	$\mathbf{79.36}_{\pm0.37}$	$87.40_{\pm0.25}$	$75.12_{\pm0.41}$	$\mathbf{80.05}_{\pm0.20}$	**80.39**
HeadAuto	$83.76_{\pm0.28}$	$74.98_{\pm0.77}$	$80.69_{\pm0.21}$	$79.01_{\pm0.27}$	$87.33_{\pm0.36}$	$\mathbf{75.66}_{\pm0.54}$	$79.98_{\pm0.10}$	80.20

Table 5: F1 scores of the (English) cross-genre experiments (averaged over 5 runs with different random seeds). "*" denotes that models are trained on the "nw*" portion. "Avg." denotes macro average over all genres.

	bc	bn	mz
BIO (w/o CRF)	$71.19_{\pm0.61}$	$77.56_{\pm0.68}$	$76.63_{\pm0.51}$
BIO (w/ CRF)	$72.11_{\pm0.98}$	$76.28_{\pm0.61}$	$75.87_{\pm0.69}$
Span	$73.30_{\pm1.07}$	$79.90_{\pm0.58}$	$77.90_{\pm0.59}$
HeadSyntax	$\mathbf{75.23}_{\pm1.00}$	$\mathbf{79.95}_{\pm0.49}$	$\mathbf{78.69}_{\pm0.41}$
HeadAuto	$73.60_{\pm0.49}$	$78.97_{\pm0.53}$	$77.60_{\pm0.41}$

Table 6: F1 scores of the (English) cross-genre experiments (averaged over 5 runs with different random seeds) on specific genres without excluding auxiliary predicates (with BERT).

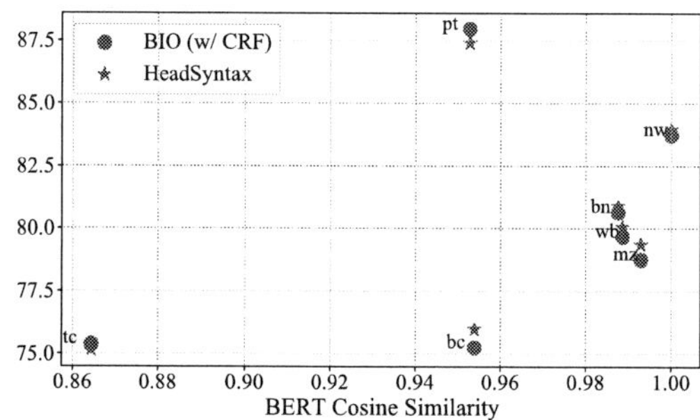

Figure 3: F1 results versus genre similarities according to BERT representations.

OntoNotes and split the corpus according to the genres. There are seven genres, including broadcast conversation (bc), broadcast news (bn), newswire (nw), magazine (mz), pivot (Bible) (pt), telephone conversation (tc) and web (wb) text. The models are trained on the newswire (nw) portion and directly evaluated on portions of all the genres. Table 5 shows the test results. The overall trends are similar to those in the fully-supervised setting. Without BERT, more span-aware structured decoders perform better by more than for 1 point compared to BIO-tagging. After including BERT features, the gaps decrease. Nevertheless, more structured decoders can still perform competitively.

Note that in this setting, we perform evaluations with a correction to an annotation inconsistency that originally favored more structured (direct) decoders. We find that there are inconsistent annotations for the predicates of auxiliary verbs across some genres, we thus exclude them[10] for evaluation. In the genres of "bc", "bn" and "mz", there are many more auxiliary verbs annotated than those in "nw". Interestingly, if not excluding these examples, the more structured decoders perform better than BIO-tagging even with BERT, as shown in Table 6. A possible explanation is that the more structured decoders usually see more negative examples during training and might be more conservative when predicting arguments for these auxiliary verbs, which do not have any arguments. On the contrary, the BIO-tagger tends to over-predict arguments in these cases, leading to worse results. Nevertheless, this phenomenon is only the result of an annotation inconsistency in the dataset and we thus exclude these auxiliary verbs from evaluation in this setting.

We further compare cross-genre results with genre (domain) similarities. Following Aharoni and Goldberg (2020), we obtain similarity scores from target genres to the source genre (nw) by calculating cosine similarity of the centroids of BERT representations. Specifically, we first compute sentence-level representations by average pooling the final hidden vectors with a vanilla BERT, then the genre-level representations are obtained by fur-

---

[10] We exclude ["be.03", "become.03", "do.01", "have.01"].

	Dev	Test
BIO (w/o CRF)	$56.73_{\pm0.63}$	$56.18_{\pm0.61}$
BIO (w/ CRF)	$56.86_{\pm1.05}$	$56.47_{\pm0.95}$
Span	$56.61_{\pm0.51}$	$55.97_{\pm0.39}$
HeadSyntax	$\mathbf{57.05}_{\pm0.36}$	$56.48_{\pm0.34}$
HeadAuto	$\mathbf{57.05}_{\pm0.59}$	$\mathbf{56.51}_{\pm0.66}$

Table 7: Unlabeled F1 scores of English→Chinese zero-shot cross-lingual experiments (averaged over five runs with different random seeds).

Gold	[你] [在 纽约 时报 上] 写 了 [一 篇 文章]
Literally	[you] [at New York Times] <u>wrote</u> [an article]
Predicted	[你] [在 纽约 时报 上] 写 [了 一 篇 文章]

Table 8: A typical error of cross-lingual systems. Here, the predicate is the <u>underlined</u> "写"(wrote) and the gold and predicted arguments are presented in [the brackets]. The cross-lingual models wrongly include the extra auxiliary word "了" in the last argument.

Decoding	Without BERT	With BERT
BIO (w/o CRF)	$709.8_{\pm10.6}$	$412.3_{\pm4.6}$
BIO (w/ CRF)	$497.0_{\pm4.5}$	$335.1_{\pm4.3}$
Span	$355.8_{\pm5.4}$	$261.3_{\pm3.7}$
HeadSyntax	$561.6_{\pm5.1}$	$372.8_{\pm4.5}$
HeadAuto	$454.9_{\pm7.9}$	$311.0_{\pm5.8}$

Table 9: Speed comparisons of decoding methods (evaluated by number of sequences per second, averaged over 5 runs, on one TITAN-RTX GPU).

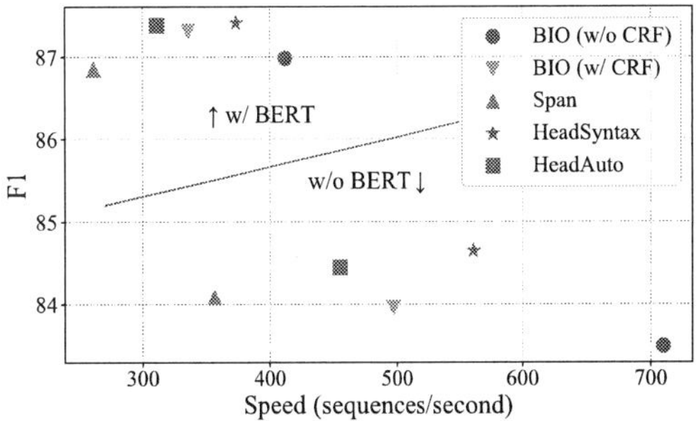

Figure 4: Comparing speed vs. F1 with different decoding methods (on CoNLL05 development set).

ther averaging all sentence-level ones in the corpus. We show the results of "BIO (w/ CRF)" and "HeadSyntax" in Figure 3. Generally, F1 scores on target genres have a weak correlation with genre similarities to the source (Pearson's correlation is 0.45). The outlier "pt" is a special case (biblical text) which mainly contains simple instances.

3.4 Cross-lingual Experiments

We further explore a simple zero-shot cross-lingual setting. We still take the CoNLL-2012 subset of the Ontonotes corpus. The models are trained on the English sets, and then directly applied to the Chinese sets. This time we exclude word embeddings and only use representations from multilingual BERT as the input features, which has shown to be effective for cross-lingual transfer (Wu and Dredze, 2019). Since the Chinese and English PropBanks use different frames, the labeled results might not be directly comparable. We thus perform unlabeled training and evaluate unlabeled argument F1 scores, which reveal how well the models extract argument spans. We simply collapse all the role labels into one special "IsArg" label.

The results are listed in Table 7. The trends are still similar to the previous monolingual experiments with BERT, different decoders obtain similar results, especially considering the deviations of multiple runs. In this setting, the CRF does not help as much as in the case of monolingual experiments. The main reason might be that we are training unlabeled systems, and the main transi-

tion that CRF is capturing is "I" after "B", which does not provide too much enhancement. Interestingly, in our preliminary experiments, we also tried labeled training, and found that the CRF is actually harmful, since the distributions of the tag transitions might be different across languages.

We further investigate the systems' outputs and find similar error patterns. Table 8 lists a typical example, where in Chinese the auxiliary word "了" (which denotes perfective aspect[11]) is incorrectly included in the argument. This error is not surprising if considering that in the English training corpus, the predicate verbs usually have directly-following arguments. All extraction methods explored in this work are unlikely to fix such errors without language-specific knowledge.

3.5 Speed Comparisons

Finally we compare the decoding speed of different extraction methods. Results are shown in Table 9 and we further compare them against F1 scores in Figure 4. Greedy BIO-tagging (w/o CRF) obtains the highest speed. However, this comes with a drop of around 0.5 F1 points without BERT and 0.3 F1 points with BERT. Although the two-step approaches require two decoding steps, they

---

[11]`https://universaldependencies.org/zh/dep/aux_.html`

are still efficient thanks to the simplicity of both steps. When trained with syntactic information, this model is the second best in terms of decoding speed. On the other hand, even with beam pruning, the span-based decoder still needs to score a number of span candidates quadratic in the input sequence length, making it less efficient compared to other decoders.

4 Related Work

Argument Extraction Before the incorporation of end-to-end neural models, traditional SRL systems usually depend on input constituency trees to obtain argument candidates (Xue and Palmer, 2004; Màrquez et al., 2008). Although straightforward, this may suffer from error propagation from syntax parsers. Recent neural systems utilize end-to-end models to solve the task. Casting SRL as BIO-based sequence labeling problem is the most common decoding scheme and can obtain impressive results (Zhou and Xu, 2015; He et al., 2017; Tan et al., 2018; Strubell et al., 2018; Shi and Lin, 2019). On the other hand, span-based methods (He et al., 2018a; Ouchi et al., 2018) directly select and label among argument span candidates. This is actually similar to the traditional approaches, though the argument candidates are obtained by the model rather than from input syntax trees. In addition to span-based SRL, the focus of this work, there is another category of dependency-style SRL, which only requires the extraction of head words of argument spans (Surdeanu et al., 2008; Hajič et al., 2009). Inspired by this, for span-based SRL, we can extract argument head words as the first step and then expand to the full spans in a second step. This idea has also been applied in information extraction, such as coreference resolution (Peng et al., 2015), entity detection (Lin et al., 2019) and event argument extraction (Zhang et al., 2020). Another interesting direction is considering the structured constraints of the arguments, including works on integer linear programming (Punyakanok et al., 2004, 2008), dynamic programming (Täckström et al., 2015) and structure-aware tuning (Li et al., 2020).

Syntax and SRL There has been discussion of the relation between syntax and SRL (Gildea and Palmer, 2002; Punyakanok et al., 2008), considering the close connections between these two tasks. Though syntax trees are usually the inputs to traditional SRL systems, some recent works find that syntax-agnostic neural models also work well (Marcheggiani et al., 2017; Cai et al., 2018). Nevertheless, with recent neural models, syntax information has still been found helpful for SRL in various ways, including multi-task learning (Swayamdipta et al., 2018; Strubell et al., 2018), argument pruning (He et al., 2018b), and tree-based modeling (Marcheggiani and Titov, 2017; Li et al., 2018; Marcheggiani and Titov, 2020). In this work, our "HeadSyntax" decoder incorporates syntax in a partial way, utilizing dependency trees to decide the head words in training. This method indeed performs the best overall if only adopting static word embeddings. However, the incorporation of BERT features diminishes the advantages. This indicates that BERT may already cover much of the syntactic (surface) features of the input sentences, as suggested by recent works on BERT interpretation (Goldberg, 2019; Hewitt and Manning, 2019; Tenney et al., 2019; Clark et al., 2019).

Cross-lingual SRL There has also been increasing interest in cross-lingual transfer for SRL, where data transfer and model transfer are the main approaches. Data transfer usually depends on translation and annotation projection to obtain training resources for target languages (Padó and Lapata, 2009; Akbik et al., 2015; Aminian et al., 2019; Fei et al., 2020a; Daza and Frank, 2020). On the other hand, model transfer techniques directly reuse an SRL model trained on source languages to transfer to target languages (Kozhevnikov and Titov, 2013; Fei et al., 2020b), based on common representations. In particular, the recent development of multilingual neural representations, such as multilingual BERT, has been shown to be effective for cross-lingual transfer (Wu and Dredze, 2019; Pires et al., 2019). In this work, we explore a simple zero-shot unlabeled setting for cross-lingual SRL. We leave more explorations on this to future work.

5 Conclusion

In this work, we empirically compare several span extraction methods for SRL. Extensive results show that in fully supervised settings, simple BIO-tagging is a robustly good option when utilizing BERT features. Similar trends are also found in cross-genre and cross-lingual settings. We also analyze the accuracy-efficiency trade-offs for different decoders; although methodologically more complex, two-step approaches are still efficient in decoding. Future work could explore other NLP tasks that require extracting textual spans.

References

Roee Aharoni and Yoav Goldberg. 2020. Unsupervised domain clusters in pretrained language models. In *Proceedings of the 58th Annual Meeting of the Association for Computational Linguistics*, pages 7747–7763, Online. Association for Computational Linguistics.

Alan Akbik, Laura Chiticariu, Marina Danilevsky, Yunyao Li, Shivakumar Vaithyanathan, and Huaiyu Zhu. 2015. Generating high quality proposition Banks for multilingual semantic role labeling. In *Proceedings of the 53rd Annual Meeting of the Association for Computational Linguistics and the 7th International Joint Conference on Natural Language Processing (Volume 1: Long Papers)*, pages 397–407, Beijing, China. Association for Computational Linguistics.

Maryam Aminian, Mohammad Sadegh Rasooli, and Mona Diab. 2019. Cross-lingual transfer of semantic roles: From raw text to semantic roles. In *Proceedings of the 13th International Conference on Computational Semantics - Long Papers*, pages 200–210, Gothenburg, Sweden. Association for Computational Linguistics.

Jiaxun Cai, Shexia He, Zuchao Li, and Hai Zhao. 2018. A full end-to-end semantic role labeler, syntactic-agnostic over syntactic-aware? In *Proceedings of the 27th International Conference on Computational Linguistics*, pages 2753–2765, Santa Fe, New Mexico, USA. Association for Computational Linguistics.

Xavier Carreras and Lluís Màrquez. 2005. Introduction to the CoNLL-2005 shared task: Semantic role labeling. In *Proceedings of the Ninth Conference on Computational Natural Language Learning (CoNLL-2005)*, pages 152–164, Ann Arbor, Michigan. Association for Computational Linguistics.

Kevin Clark, Urvashi Khandelwal, Omer Levy, and Christopher D. Manning. 2019. What does BERT look at? an analysis of BERT's attention. In *Proceedings of the 2019 ACL Workshop BlackboxNLP: Analyzing and Interpreting Neural Networks for NLP*, pages 276–286, Florence, Italy. Association for Computational Linguistics.

Angel Daza and Anette Frank. 2020. X-SRL: A parallel cross-lingual semantic role labeling dataset. In *Proceedings of the 2020 Conference on Empirical Methods in Natural Language Processing (EMNLP)*, pages 3904–3914, Online. Association for Computational Linguistics.

Jacob Devlin, Ming-Wei Chang, Kenton Lee, and Kristina Toutanova. 2019. BERT: Pre-training of deep bidirectional transformers for language understanding. In *Proceedings of the 2019 Conference of the North American Chapter of the Association for Computational Linguistics: Human Language Technologies, Volume 1 (Long and Short Papers)*, pages 4171–4186, Minneapolis, Minnesota. Association for Computational Linguistics.

Hao Fei, Meishan Zhang, and Donghong Ji. 2020a. Cross-lingual semantic role labeling with high-quality translated training corpus. In *Proceedings of the 58th Annual Meeting of the Association for Computational Linguistics*, pages 7014–7026, Online. Association for Computational Linguistics.

Hao Fei, Meishan Zhang, Fei Li, and Donghong Ji. 2020b. Cross-lingual semantic role labeling with model transfer. *IEEE/ACM Transactions on Audio, Speech, and Language Processing*, 28:2427–2437.

Daniel Gildea and Daniel Jurafsky. 2002. Automatic labeling of semantic roles. *Computational Linguistics*, 28(3):245–288.

Daniel Gildea and Martha Palmer. 2002. The necessity of parsing for predicate argument recognition. In *Proceedings of the 40th Annual Meeting of the Association for Computational Linguistics*, pages 239–246, Philadelphia, Pennsylvania, USA. Association for Computational Linguistics.

Yoav Goldberg. 2019. Assessing bert's syntactic abilities. *arXiv preprint arXiv:1901.05287*.

Jan Hajič, Massimiliano Ciaramita, Richard Johansson, Daisuke Kawahara, Maria Antònia Martí, Lluís Màrquez, Adam Meyers, Joakim Nivre, Sebastian Padó, Jan Štěpánek, Pavel Straňák, Mihai Surdeanu, Nianwen Xue, and Yi Zhang. 2009. The CoNLL-2009 shared task: Syntactic and semantic dependencies in multiple languages. In *Proceedings of the Thirteenth Conference on Computational Natural Language Learning (CoNLL 2009): Shared Task*, pages 1–18, Boulder, Colorado. Association for Computational Linguistics.

Luheng He, Kenton Lee, Omer Levy, and Luke Zettlemoyer. 2018a. Jointly predicting predicates and arguments in neural semantic role labeling. In *Proceedings of the 56th Annual Meeting of the Association for Computational Linguistics (Volume 2: Short Papers)*, pages 364–369, Melbourne, Australia. Association for Computational Linguistics.

Luheng He, Kenton Lee, Mike Lewis, and Luke Zettlemoyer. 2017. Deep semantic role labeling: What works and what's next. In *Proceedings of the 55th Annual Meeting of the Association for Computational Linguistics (Volume 1: Long Papers)*, pages 473–483, Vancouver, Canada. Association for Computational Linguistics.

Shexia He, Zuchao Li, Hai Zhao, and Hongxiao Bai. 2018b. Syntax for semantic role labeling, to be, or not to be. In *Proceedings of the 56th Annual Meeting of the Association for Computational Linguistics (Volume 1: Long Papers)*, pages 2061–2071, Melbourne, Australia. Association for Computational Linguistics.

John Hewitt and Christopher D. Manning. 2019. A structural probe for finding syntax in word representations. In *Proceedings of the 2019 Conference* of the North American Chapter of the Association for Computational Linguistics: Human Language Technologies, Volume 1 (Long and Short Papers), pages 4129–4138, Minneapolis, Minnesota. Association for Computational Linguistics.

Diederik P Kingma and Jimmy Ba. 2014. Adam: A method for stochastic optimization. *arXiv preprint arXiv:1412.6980*.

Mikhail Kozhevnikov and Ivan Titov. 2013. Cross-lingual transfer of semantic role labeling models. In *Proceedings of the 51st Annual Meeting of the Association for Computational Linguistics (Volume 1: Long Papers)*, pages 1190–1200, Sofia, Bulgaria. Association for Computational Linguistics.

John D Lafferty, Andrew McCallum, and Fernando CN Pereira. 2001. Conditional random fields: Probabilistic models for segmenting and labeling sequence data. In *Proceedings of the Eighteenth International Conference on Machine Learning*, pages 282–289.

Tao Li, Parth Anand Jawale, Martha Palmer, and Vivek Srikumar. 2020. Structured tuning for semantic role labeling. In *Proceedings of the 58th Annual Meeting of the Association for Computational Linguistics*, pages 8402–8412, Online. Association for Computational Linguistics.

Zuchao Li, Shexia He, Jiaxun Cai, Zhuosheng Zhang, Hai Zhao, Gongshen Liu, Linlin Li, and Luo Si. 2018. A unified syntax-aware framework for semantic role labeling. In *Proceedings of the 2018 Conference on Empirical Methods in Natural Language Processing*, pages 2401–2411, Brussels, Belgium. Association for Computational Linguistics.

Hongyu Lin, Yaojie Lu, Xianpei Han, and Le Sun. 2019. Sequence-to-nuggets: Nested entity mention detection via anchor-region networks. In *Proceedings of the 57th Annual Meeting of the Association for Computational Linguistics*, pages 5182–5192, Florence, Italy. Association for Computational Linguistics.

Christopher D Manning, Mihai Surdeanu, John Bauer, Jenny Rose Finkel, Steven Bethard, and David Mc-Closky. 2014. The stanford corenlp natural language processing toolkit. In *Proceedings of 52nd annual meeting of the association for computational linguistics: system demonstrations*, pages 55–60.

Diego Marcheggiani, Anton Frolov, and Ivan Titov. 2017. A simple and accurate syntax-agnostic neural model for dependency-based semantic role labeling. In *Proceedings of the 21st Conference on Computational Natural Language Learning (CoNLL 2017)*, pages 411–420, Vancouver, Canada. Association for Computational Linguistics.

Diego Marcheggiani and Ivan Titov. 2017. Encoding sentences with graph convolutional networks for semantic role labeling. In *Proceedings of the 2017 Conference on Empirical Methods in Natural Language Processing*, pages 1506–1515, Copenhagen, Denmark. Association for Computational Linguistics.

Diego Marcheggiani and Ivan Titov. 2020. Graph convolutions over constituent trees for syntax-aware semantic role labeling. In *Proceedings of the 2020 Conference on Empirical Methods in Natural Language Processing (EMNLP)*, pages 3915–3928, Online. Association for Computational Linguistics.

Lluís Màrquez, Xavier Carreras, Kenneth C. Litkowski, and Suzanne Stevenson. 2008. Special issue introduction: Semantic role labeling: An introduction to the special issue. *Computational Linguistics*, 34(2):145–159.

Tomas Mikolov, Edouard Grave, Piotr Bojanowski, Christian Puhrsch, and Armand Joulin. 2018. Advances in pre-training distributed word representations. In *Proceedings of the International Conference on Language Resources and Evaluation (LREC 2018)*.

Joakim Nivre, Marie-Catherine de Marneffe, Filip Ginter, Jan Hajič, Christopher D. Manning, Sampo Pyysalo, Sebastian Schuster, Francis Tyers, and Daniel Zeman. 2020. Universal Dependencies v2: An evergrowing multilingual treebank collection. In *Proceedings of the 12th Language Resources and Evaluation Conference*, pages 4034–4043, Marseille, France. European Language Resources Association.

Hiroki Ouchi, Hiroyuki Shindo, and Yuji Matsumoto. 2018. A span selection model for semantic role labeling. In *Proceedings of the 2018 Conference on Empirical Methods in Natural Language Processing*, pages 1630–1642, Brussels, Belgium. Association for Computational Linguistics.

Sebastian Padó and Mirella Lapata. 2009. Cross-lingual annotation projection for semantic roles. *Journal of Artificial Intelligence Research*, 36:307–340.

Martha Palmer, Daniel Gildea, and Nianwen Xue. 2010. Semantic role labeling. *Synthesis Lectures on Human Language Technologies*, 3(1):1–103.

Haoruo Peng, Kai-Wei Chang, and Dan Roth. 2015. A joint framework for coreference resolution and mention head detection. In *Proceedings of the Nineteenth Conference on Computational Natural Language Learning*, pages 12–21, Beijing, China. Association for Computational Linguistics.

Telmo Pires, Eva Schlinger, and Dan Garrette. 2019. How multilingual is multilingual BERT? In *Proceedings of the 57th Annual Meeting of the Association for Computational Linguistics*, pages 4996–5001, Florence, Italy. Association for Computational Linguistics.

Sameer Pradhan, Alessandro Moschitti, Nianwen Xue, Hwee Tou Ng, Anders Björkelund, Olga Uryupina, Yuchen Zhang, and Zhi Zhong. 2013. Towards robust linguistic analysis using OntoNotes. In *Proceedings of the Seventeenth Conference on Computational Natural Language Learning*, pages 143–152, Sofia, Bulgaria. Association for Computational Linguistics.

Vasin Punyakanok, Dan Roth, and Wen-tau Yih. 2008. The importance of syntactic parsing and inference in semantic role labeling. *Computational Linguistics*, 34(2):257–287.

Vasin Punyakanok, Dan Roth, Wen-tau Yih, and Dav Zimak. 2004. Semantic role labeling via integer linear programming inference. In *COLING 2004: Proceedings of the 20th International Conference on Computational Linguistics*, pages 1346–1352, Geneva, Switzerland. COLING.

Lance A Ramshaw and Mitchell P Marcus. 1999. Text chunking using transformation-based learning. In *Natural language processing using very large corpora*, pages 157–176. Springer.

Peter Shaw, Jakob Uszkoreit, and Ashish Vaswani. 2018. Self-attention with relative position representations. In *Proceedings of the 2018 Conference of the North American Chapter of the Association for Computational Linguistics: Human Language Technologies, Volume 2 (Short Papers)*, pages 464–468, New Orleans, Louisiana. Association for Computational Linguistics.

Peng Shi and Jimmy Lin. 2019. Simple bert models for relation extraction and semantic role labeling. *arXiv preprint arXiv:1904.05255*.

Emma Strubell, Patrick Verga, Daniel Andor, David Weiss, and Andrew McCallum. 2018. Linguistically-informed self-attention for semantic role labeling. In *Proceedings of the 2018 Conference on Empirical Methods in Natural Language Processing*, pages 5027–5038, Brussels, Belgium. Association for Computational Linguistics.

Mihai Surdeanu, Richard Johansson, Adam Meyers, Lluís Màrquez, and Joakim Nivre. 2008. The CoNLL 2008 shared task on joint parsing of syntactic and semantic dependencies. In *CoNLL 2008: Proceedings of the Twelfth Conference on Computational Natural Language Learning*, pages 159–177, Manchester, England. Coling 2008 Organizing Committee.

Swabha Swayamdipta, Sam Thomson, Kenton Lee, Luke Zettlemoyer, Chris Dyer, and Noah A. Smith. 2018. Syntactic scaffolds for semantic structures. In *Proceedings of the 2018 Conference on Empirical Methods in Natural Language Processing*, pages 3772–3782, Brussels, Belgium. Association for Computational Linguistics.

Oscar Täckström, Kuzman Ganchev, and Dipanjan Das. 2015. Efficient inference and structured learning for semantic role labeling. *Transactions of the Association for Computational Linguistics*, 3:29–41.

Zhixing Tan, Mingxuan Wang, Jun Xie, Yidong Chen, and Xiaodong Shi. 2018. Deep semantic role labeling with self-attention. In *Proceedings of the AAAI Conference on Artificial Intelligence*.

Ian Tenney, Dipanjan Das, and Ellie Pavlick. 2019. BERT rediscovers the classical NLP pipeline. In *Proceedings of the 57th Annual Meeting of the Association for Computational Linguistics*, pages 4593–4601, Florence, Italy. Association for Computational Linguistics.

Ashish Vaswani, Noam Shazeer, Niki Parmar, Jakob Uszkoreit, Llion Jones, Aidan N Gomez, Łukasz Kaiser, and Illia Polosukhin. 2017. Attention is all you need. In *Advances in neural information processing systems*, pages 5998–6008.

Shuohang Wang and Jing Jiang. 2016. Machine comprehension using match-lstm and answer pointer. *arXiv preprint arXiv:1608.07905*.

Shijie Wu and Mark Dredze. 2019. Beto, bentz, becas: The surprising cross-lingual effectiveness of BERT. In *Proceedings of the 2019 Conference on Empirical Methods in Natural Language Processing and the 9th International Joint Conference on Natural Language Processing (EMNLP-IJCNLP)*, pages 833–844, Hong Kong, China. Association for Computational Linguistics.

Nianwen Xue and Martha Palmer. 2004. Calibrating features for semantic role labeling. In *Proceedings of the 2004 Conference on Empirical Methods in Natural Language Processing*, pages 88–94, Barcelona, Spain. Association for Computational Linguistics.

Zhisong Zhang, Xiang Kong, Zhengzhong Liu, Xuezhe Ma, and Eduard Hovy. 2020. A two-step approach for implicit event argument detection. In *Proceedings of the 58th Annual Meeting of the Association for Computational Linguistics*, pages 7479–7485, Online. Association for Computational Linguistics.

Jie Zhou and Wei Xu. 2015. End-to-end learning of semantic role labeling using recurrent neural networks. In *Proceedings of the 53rd Annual Meeting of the Association for Computational Linguistics and the 7th International Joint Conference on Natural Language Processing (Volume 1: Long Papers)*, pages 1127–1137, Beijing, China. Association for Computational Linguistics.

Author Index